Praise for *Six Rules for Brand Revitalization*

"The six rules for brand revitalization have been validated in a number of key turnarounds. They are indispensable in today's recessionary times. A must read for every manager who confronts declining brand sales and profitability."

—**Jerry Wind**, The Lauder Professor and Professor of Marketing,
The Wharton School, University of Pennsylvania

"The automotive retail industry has been trying hard to change more than a half century of negative image caused by some tradition of customer-unfriendly practices and unfavorable media coverage. We have combined Larry's branding concept and his six rules with our company's customer-first heritage and are making significant progress."

—**Shau-Wai Lam**, Chairman and CEO,
DCH Auto Group

"Light tells the story of the McDonald's revitalization in a way that makes it seem like you were there. With his depth of experience and insight, he extracts principles that are applicable in any situation. If your brand is stagnating or in decline, this is a MUST read."

—**David J. Reibstein**, The William S. Woodside Professor and
Professor of Marketing, The Wharton School University of Pennsylvania

"Larry and Joan have laid out a great set of guiding principles for any business executive—whether they are revitalizing a brand or making sure it stays relevant."

—**Russ Smyth**, CEO, H&R Block;
former President, McDonald's Europe

"Brand revitalization—impossible to accomplish without the Executive Suite's overriding desire for a strong/clear brand platform and execution of the brand that recognizes the company's potential for risk and rewards.

"Management must have the ability to not only possess the vision but allow and encourage others to express the brand through many of the touch-points to customers, employees, vendors, and the media. It's fundamentally important to realize that although management should be the steward (caretaker) of the brand, it's not the sole owner."

—**Steve Bagby**, President,
BAGBY ideas >360°, Chicago, Illinois

"Having worked with Larry and Joan while I headed M&M/Mars, I am delighted they have finally written a book encapsulating their principles and processes. This book demonstrates the fundamental truth that brand building begins with understanding changing consumer wants. Creating, building, maintaining, and strengthening consumer relevance is the key to brand success. This book is a gift for those who believe in brands and know that marketing is bigger than just advertising. This is a delightful read...I could not put it down."

—**Howard Walker**, former President,
M&M/Mars

"Over the past two years, Larry has been a great partner in transforming our organization to a more customer-centric one. His insights on how to align employees' motivations and capabilities to marketing strategy will be invaluable to any senior management team embarking on a major turnaround initiative or embarking on a customer-driven growth journey."

—**Vincenzo Picone**, Global Chief Marketing Officer,
GE Capital

SIX RULES FOR

Brand
Revitalization

Learn How Companies
Like McDonald's Can
Re-Energize Their Brands

Larry Light and Joan Kiddon,
Arcature LLC

Vice President, Publisher: Tim Moore
Associate Publisher and Director of Marketing: Amy Neidlinger
Wharton Editor: Steve Kobrin
Editorial Assistant: Pamela Boland
Development Editor: Russ Hall
Operations Manager: Gina Kanouse
Digital Marketing Manager: Julie Phifer
Publicity Manager: Laura Czaja
Assistant Marketing Manager: Megan Colvin
Cover Designer: Alan Clements
Managing Editor: Kristy Hart
Project Editor: Anne Goebel
Copy Editor: Geneil Breeze
Proofreader: Water Crest Publishing
Indexer: Lisa Stumpf
Compositor: Nonie Ratcliff
Manufacturing Buyer: Dan Uhrig

Wharton School Publishing offers excellent discounts on this book when ordered in quantity
for bulk purchases or special sales. For more information, please contact U.S. Corporate and
Government Sales, 1-800-382-3419, corpsales@pearsontechgroup.com. For sales outside the
U.S., please contact International Sales at international@pearson.com.

Printed in the United States of America

First Printing February 2009

ISBN-10: 0-13-604331-3
ISBN-13: 978-0-13-604331-7

Pearson Education LTD.
Pearson Education Australia PTY, Limited.
Pearson Education Singapore, Pte. Ltd.
Pearson Education North Asia, Ltd.
Pearson Education Canada, Ltd.
Pearson Educatión de Mexico, S.A. de C.V.
Pearson Education—Japan
Pearson Education Malaysia, Pte. Ltd.

Light, Marvin Lawrence, 1941-
    Six rules for brand revitalization : learn how companies like McDonald's can re-energize their
brands / Marvin Lawrence Light, Joan S. Kiddon. -- 1st ed.
        p. cm.
    ISBN 0-13-604331-3 (hardback : alk. paper)
    1. Branding (Marketing)—Management. 2. Brand name
products--Management. 3. Product life cycle. 4. McDonald's
Corporation--Case studies. I. Kiddon, Joan S., 1949- II. Title. III.
Title: Brand revitalization: learn how companies like McDonald's can re-energize their brands.
    HF5415.1255.L54 2009
    658.8'27--dc22
                        2008034733

We dedicate this book to the memories and the leadership of both Jim and Charlie, who loved the McDonald's brand with passion and who lived the McDonald's brand with pride.
—Larry Light and Joan Kiddon

Contents

Acknowledgments

This book would not have been possible without the encouragement and support of professors George Day, David Reibstein, and Yoram (Jerry) Wind. They believed that the McDonald's turnaround was not only a great business case but the basis for a business leadership book. Our sincerest thanks go to our editor Martha Cooley who more than once helped us to find the best way to put all the pieces together, and to our project editor Anne Goebel who had extraordinary patience shepherding us through the editing process with tact and graciousness. Special thanks goes to our colleague here at Arcature LLC, Margaret Phillips, who helped us keep the business running as we wrote. And, of course, we want to thank our families for continuing to put up with us and love us... Joyce, Laura, and Michelle Light, and Chloé and Olivia Kiddon, and Naomi Levine.

About the Authors

Larry Light is CEO of Arcature LLC, a leading global brand consultant. He served as Global Chief Marketing Officer for McDonald's during 2002-2005, the crucial years of its marketing turnaround. Working with organizations ranging from Nissan, 3M, to IBM, he has developed breakthrough principles, concepts, techniques, and processes for nurturing, managing, and building brands for enduring profitable growth. Light was formerly Executive Vice-President at BBDO, responsible for market research and media; Chairman and CEO of the international division of Bates Worldwide; and a member of Bates' Board of Directors.

Joan Kiddon is president and COO of Arcature LLC. She consulted on McDonald's key strategic projects during the brand turnaround. Kiddon began her marketing career at BBDO in New York, moving to BBDO/West in Los Angeles where she was the Director of Market Research. After several years as an independent consultant, she joined Arcature LLC in 1991.

Preface

In 1998, McDonald's hired Arcature LLC, our consulting firm, to help develop a global brand direction. The client was Charlie Bell, the Managing Director of McDonald's Australia and Asia/Pacific region. Charlie's career advanced quickly, and he soon became President of the International Division of McDonald's. He asked us to lead a project to refine and help implement the global brand direction. But because of various organizational and cultural roadblocks, the recommended strategy did not get implemented. In 2002, at the biannual operator convention, Jack Greenberg, who was the McDonald's CEO at the time, observed that, "Marketing is broken at McDonald's."[1] He announced that McDonald's was initiating a search for a Global Chief Marketing Officer. After several months of searching for a candidate, Charlie Bell called. Using his true Aussie charm, Charlie asked, "How would you like to put into practice what you preach? Join the team and help us to turn around this business. This is a great opportunity to demonstrate that what you say works. Unlike most consultants, you would be accountable for implementation and the results." Few consultants have this opportunity. I accepted the challenge.

I had worked in the advertising business as the Chairman and CEO of the international division of Bates Worldwide and was a member of the Bates Board of Directors. Prior to Bates, I spent 16 years at BBDO in New York, becoming the Executive Vice President responsible for both marketing and media.

Over the years, working on both the agency and the consulting sides of marketing, I developed strong viewpoints, principles, concepts, techniques, and processes for nurturing, managing, and building brands for enduring profitable growth. Based on my experience

---

[1] *PROMO* magazine, April 29, 2002, http://promomagazine.com/news/marketing_mcdonalds_seeks_exec/.

with brands such as Nissan, Post-it notes, IBM, *The New York Times*, McDonald's, and others, I became interested in the profitable growth opportunity of brand revitalization. The opportunity at McDonald's gave me the chance to put these ideas into practice firsthand.

Even though the McDonald's business was showing signs of weakness, I shared Charlie's conviction that the McDonald's brand could be revitalized. There was no question in my mind that with the brand's reservoir of goodwill, and with a refocus on the potential of a revitalized McDonald's brand, the business could be restored to enduring profitable growth. My belief in rejuvenating the McDonald's brand was a constant theme from the moment in July 2002 that Charlie Bell called about the global CMO appointment.

At the end of 2002, an article about McDonald's appeared with the title, "Hamburger Hell."[2] I still remember the cover artwork with its dark, menacing flames. This was not the only one of its kind. Article after article described the unfortunate conditions of McDonald's. Reporters, analysts, observers, activists, franchisees, employees, marketing consultants, everyone had something negative to say: McDonald's was "out of date"; "too large to be turned around"; "Its time is passed."[3]

A little more than one year later, as I spoke before a meeting hosted by *The Economist* magazine in March 2004, I opened my speech by quoting different headlines: "The Sizzle is Back"; "Eye Popping Performance"; and "McDonald's Leaves Analysts Upbeat on

---

[2] Gogoi, Pallavi and Arndt, Michael, "Hamburger Hell," *BusinessWeek*, March 3, 2003.

[3] Articles such as these were appearing: Browning, E. S. and Gibson, Richard, "McDonald's Arches Lose Golden Luster," *The Wall Street Journal*, September 3, 1997; Leonhardt, David, "McDonald's: Can It Regain Its Golden Touch?" *BusinessWeek*, March 9, 1998; Tatge, Mark and Copple, Brandon, "McMissteps," *Forbes* December 10, 2001.

Prospects."[4] And, after another year, McDonald's was being described as an incredible turnaround business case.[5]

In a conference call hosted by David Palmer of UBS, he said the McDonald's turnaround is "one of the great brand recoveries in corporate history."[6] The financial web site, The Motley Fool, observed that "The world's largest fast food chain has reinvented itself and spruced up its income statements thanks to the late Jim Cantalupo."[7]

In October 2004, a Piper Jaffray report headlined, "Victory Lap for Plan to Win." The report went on to observe, "Aided by its Plan to Win, MCD posted a worldwide same-store sales gain of 5.8%, fueled by a domestic 8.5% jump. Defying what few critics remain, MCDs domestic base continues to produce best-in-class same-store sales aided by a sustained program to catapult the business to the next level."[8]

Over the years, we have developed processes, principles, and concepts to help revitalize brands. That is the story of this book.

The brand turnaround was a highly disciplined operation. We had a well-organized process. We followed a focused, controlled plan. But, this is not just a story about the revitalization of McDonald's. Several important lessons from this experience can and do apply to a wide variety of situations, including business to business, services, as well as consumer products.

---

[4] Articles about the McDonald's recovery started appearing as early as April 2003: Buckley, Neil, "McDonald's Back to Black," *The Financial Times*, April 29, 2003; Lambert, Emily, "Arches Turn Golden Again," Makers & Breakers column, *Forbes*, September 1, 2003; Buckley, Neil, "McDonald's Beefs Up Sales," *The Financial Times*, July 30, 2003; Leung, Shirley, "McDonald's Net Increases 12.5%, Bolstered by Strong US Sales," *The Wall Street Journal*, October 12, 2003.

[5] By December 11, 2007, as the brand continued to reap the effects of the Cantalupo/Bell turnaround, McDonald's stock hit an all-time high of 63.13. www.wsj.com historical charting.

[6] David Palmer, UBS conference call, September 2004.

[7] The Motley Fool, October 15, 2004, www.fool.com.

[8] Piper Jaffray, Analysts' report, Company note: Oakes, Peter H., CFA, Sr. Research Analyst and Scott R. Waltmann, Research Analyst, October 20, 2004.

I had the great pleasure to work with two extraordinary business executives, Jim Cantalupo, CEO, and Charlie Bell, COO, who became my very good friend. With Jim's untimely death at the Owner-Operator Convention in April 2004, Charlie became the company's youngest CEO. Soon after Charlie's appointment, he died, too. It was a heart-wrenching experience for me as it was for everyone.

In addition to the leadership of Jim and Charlie, Matt Paull, the Chief Financial Officer, was an important early supporter on the leadership team. He was a passionate believer that revitalizing the McDonald's brand was critical to enduring profitable growth. Also, I had a terrific global team of brand marketers led by Dean Barrett and Jackie Woodward.

Turning around the McDonald's brand was an incredible business experience. My three years at McDonald's were exhilarating and emotionally draining. There were the highs of launching McDonald's first-ever common brand direction worldwide campaign in 119 countries. There were the lows of the sudden deaths of my two most important supporters, Charlie Bell and Jim Cantalupo.

This book is not just mine but theirs as well. Above all, the new brand direction—at the core of the turnaround—would not have been as successful without both Jim's and Charlie's unwavering support. I base this book not only on recollections but also on the well-documented publicly available information about McDonald's. There are a lot of versions of the turnaround. Some are accurate and some are not. So, aside from the lessons that can be learned from the actions that were taken to revitalize the McDonald's brand from 2003 to 2005, this book is also a chance to describe what really happened as McDonald's went from hell to well.

—Larry Light

Introduction to the Rules and the Rules-Based Practices

The plan of this book is to share the Arcature principles and practices that contributed to several brand turnarounds, including McDonald's. I structured the book around the Six Rules of Revitalization. These are the guiding principles for rejuvenating a brand and creating a brand revitalization mindset. Within each Rule are the practices we followed. Rules are important: They provide the beliefs, commitments, learning, and framework that bring thinking to life. But rules without actions are theory without throughput.

The book's structure is shown in Figure 0.1. The driver for brand revitalization, as for all brand building is enduring profitable growth. We must have growth—grow or die, some say—but that growth must be both profitable and enduring. This means that we must have more customers who buy or visit more often who are more loyal and are more profitable.

Using these Rules and the rules-based practices embedded within, brand owners, brand managers, and brand teams will see how to revitalize a brand while generating a brand revitalization-centric mindset. I use the McDonald's story, as well as other examples to illustrate and demonstrate how this can be a winning approach.

To begin, I believe it is essential to recreate and share the context that existed and precipitated the McDonald's revival.

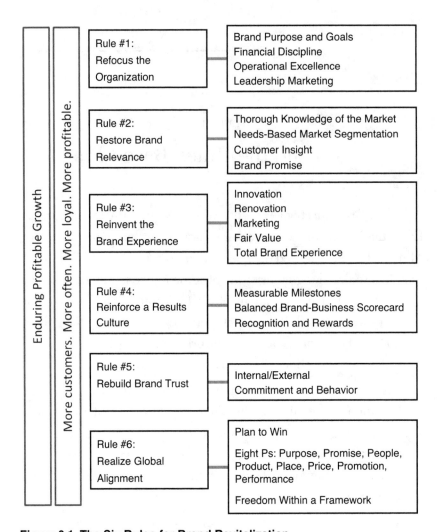

Figure 0.1 The Six Rules for Brand Revitalization

1

Background to the Turnaround

Big Brand in Big Trouble

In February 1996, McDonald's stock traded at 27 times earnings. But in July 1997, McDonald's second quarter profit growth was just 4%, with a 2% decline in earnings from the US business.

When I joined McDonald's in September 2002, the stock price was down to $17.66 from a high of $45.31 in March 1999. McDonald's reported its first-ever quarterly loss of $344 million since it went public in 1965, with same-store sales down 1.9% in Europe, 6.1% in Asia-Pacific, and 1.4 % in the United States.[1]

In December 2002, after McDonald's stock declined 60% over three years, the board of directors replaced Jack Greenberg with Jim Cantalupo as CEO, who they wooed out of retirement. Jim was a McDonald's veteran who had led the international division beginning in 1987. By March 12, 2003, the stock price was just above $12.[2]

---

[1] The Associated Press (AP), December 17, 2002.

[2] *The Wall Street Journal*, Stock Charting, historical quotes, Dow Jones & Company, Inc., http://online.wsj.com/public/quotes/main.html?symbol=MCD+mod=moj_companies+type=djn.

McDonald's sales were in decline, market share was shrinking, franchisees were frustrated, employee morale was low, and customer satisfaction was even lower.[3] The loss column was full.

On the plus side, McDonald's had one great asset: Consumers had truly fond memories of their McDonald's brand experience. People recalled their happy experiences at McDonald's as a child. Parents remembered their parents taking them to McDonald's. Unfortunately, this great asset was not generating great profits: The problem was that the majority of consumers did not have recent fond experiences.

What Went Wrong?

Many things contributed to the decline of the McDonald's brand between 1997 and 2002. It was not a precipitous fall: The brand had been declining slowly, painfully, and publicly for some time. The simplest analysis of what went wrong is that McDonald's violated the three brand-building basics for enduring profitable growth:

- Renovation
- Innovation
- Marketing

---

[3] The business press had been tracking the McDonald's decline for some time. A prescient article in *Business Week* ran on October 21, 1991, titled "McRisky" by Lois Therrin. Another *Business Week* article in the March 17, 1997 issue by Greg Burns had the headline "McDonald's: Now It's Just Like Any Other Burger Joint." In that article, Damon Brundage of NatWest Securities Corp. said, "They have transformed one of the great brands in American business into a commodity." Other articles critiqued the tactics and the marketing such as "Same Old, Same Old," *Forbes*, Copple, Brandon, February 19, 2001; "McDonald's Is Missing the Mark," *BrandWeek*, Miller, David, November 12, 2001.

Three Basics for Enduring Profitable Growth

- Renovation
- Innovation
- Marketing

Reckitt Benckiser is the world's biggest maker of household cleaning products. Up to 40% of its sales are generated by products that are less than three years old. Bart Becht, the CEO, says that the company's success is due to a culture that is innovative and entrepreneurial.[4]

McDonald's failed to continuously improve its brand experience by ignoring these three criticalities: renovation, innovation, and marketing. Instead, McDonald's focused on cost reduction instead of quality growth of the top line.

When the image of the brand was deteriorating, instead of investing in brand experience renovations and innovations, McDonald's focused on monthly promotions rather than on brand building. Instead of brand building marketing communications, the focus was on monthly promotional tactics designed to drive short-term sales at the expense of brand equity.[5] One member of my global team called this the "fireworks" approach to marketing: big bursts of activities that dissipated quickly.

As a result, between 1997 and 2002, we witnessed the sad decline of a mismanaged and mismarketed brand. The brand misery was

---

[4] *The Economist*, "Cleaning Up," February 16, 2008.

[5] *PROMO* magazine, April 29, 2002, "One McDonald's executive said the chain has too many marketing messages 'cluttering the airwaves and minds of its customers,'" http://promomagazine.com/news/marketing_mcdonalds_seeks_exec/.

played out in the press.[6] One analyst saw a faltering brand that was lacking in food quality, pleasant service, and helpful employees.[7] Mark Kalinowski at Salomon Smith Barney was highly critical of the management of the McDonald's brand, and in response to management's briefing on revamping the exteriors of the restaurants, he said, "Having a better looking building does nothing to fix rude service, slow service, or inaccurate order fulfillment."[8]

There were some bright spots, such as France. Under the leadership of Denis Hennequin, menu modifications and redesigned interiors brought customers into the restaurants. In Australia, Charlie Bell's idea of McCafé offered quality coffee, tea, and pastries in a quieter, more attractive atmosphere. Whether a complete McCafé, or a more limited coffee offering, the Australian experience proved that improving McDonald's coffee quality and variety has a positive effect on sales. It takes effort to revitalize a big, mature brand like McDonald's. It also took a lot of effort to sabotage this great brand. To set the context for the massive revitalization, here are some of the strategies and activities and the thinking behind those initiatives that helped to send the brand on its downward spin.

Ready, Set, Open

As same-store sales declined, McDonald's focused on building new stores as the primary growth strategy. Instead of increasing the

---

[6] Carpenter, Dave, "McDonald's Stock Hits 7-Year Low," AP, September 20, 2002; "McDonald's Warns on Profits, Stock Tumbles 13%," Reuters, September 17, 2002; Foster, Julie, "You Deserve a Better Break Today," *BusinessWeek*, September 30, 2002; Leung, Shirley, "McDonald's to Serve Up First Loss," *The Wall Street Journal*, December 18, 2002; Buckley, Neil, "McDonald's Posts Loss, Cuts Growth Target," *The Financial Times*, January 24, 2003; "McDonald's Stock Fall to 9-Year Low, AP, February 13, 2003.

[7] Kalinowski, Mark, Salomon Smith Barney, September 9, 2002.

[8] Chu, Vivian, "McDonald's Warns on Profits; Stock Tumbles 13%," Reuters, September 17, 2002.

number of customers visiting existing stores, McDonald's focused on increasing the number of stores. The major strategic road to growth was to open new restaurants, open new countries, and generate traffic with the fireworks of monthly tactical promotions and price deals. At an analysts briefing, Michael Quinlan, then chairman and CEO, said in January 1998, "You can look for about 2,200 worldwide and maybe 350 net new restaurants in the US…" as restaurant expansion plans for 1998 are likely to replicate last year's.[9] This projected rate of expansion is approximately equivalent to a new store opening every four hours.

Even as the company increased the number of restaurants by about 50% over ten years, market share declined.[10] Yet, CEO Jack Greenberg continued the growth strategy based on the rapid opening of new stores. Due to this focus on expansion over organic growth, franchisees reported that revenues and profits per existing store were cannibalized. For every new McDonald's that opened, franchisees reported that nearby stores lost between 6% and 20% of their revenues. McDonald's reported six quarters of earnings decline in 2001 and 2002.

There are consequences to overzealous expansion as a growth strategy. It was not possible to properly staff and train people to provide a quality McDonald's experience at this rate of store openings. Service suffered because people had to be trained too quickly. The focus changes to efficiency at the expense of effectiveness. You lose your connection to your core promise as you race to ribbon-cuttings.

McDonald's was at the bottom of the fast food industry on the University of Michigan survey of customer satisfaction.[11] In a 2001

---

[9] Gibson, Richard, *The Wall Street Journal*, January 23, 1998.

[10] Leonhardt, David, "McDonald's: Can It Regain Its Golden Touch," *BusinessWeek*, March 9, 1998.

[11] American Customer Satisfaction Index, University of Michigan, historical scores, www.theacsi.org

survey conducted by Sandelman and Associates, McDonald's came last among 60 fast food brands in terms of food quality ratings.[12]

Not surprisingly, the declining performance of McDonald's demoralized the franchisees. According to Reggie Webb, who operated 11 McDonald's restaurants in Los Angeles, "From my perspective, I am working harder than ever and making less than I ever had on an average-store basis."[13] Regular evaluations showed that the quality of the brand experience declined. The declining measures of these factors demoralized the system. So, McDonald's decided to discontinue the practice of regular store evaluations. Mike Roberts, head of McDonald's USA, revived the measurement program in the United States in 2002. Later, McDonald's expanded this measurement program around the world.[14]

Starbucks is a good example of what can happen when you lose that connection to your brand experience. As an unintended consequence of growing too fast, the distinctive experience of the Starbuck's brand became diluted. Howard Schultz returned as CEO of Starbucks.[15] He committed himself and the organization to restoring the unique customer experience of Starbucks.

As McDonald's focused on building more stores, consumers were demanding better food, better choices, better service, and better restaurant ambiance. McDonald's took its eye off the goal of making the brand better and focused on merely making the brand bigger.

---

[12] Eisenberg, Daniel, "Can McDonald's Shape Up?," www.time.com, 2002.

[13] Gogoi, Pallavi and Arndt, Michael, "Hamburger Hell," *BusinessWeek*, March 3, 2003.

[14] Garber, Amy, "No mystery: shopping the shops gains in popularity," Nation's Restaurant News, December 13, 2004.

[15] In first quarter 2008, Starbucks began a revitalization of the brand, bringing Howard Schultz back, eliminating noncoffee items, and closing the restaurants one evening in February for a retraining/inspiration internal marketing event, namely: *The New York Times*, January 30, 2008; *The New York Times*, January 31, 2008; *The Wall Street Journal*, January 31, 2008, as examples.

Buying and Modifying

Inside the hallways at Oak Brook, Illinois, some members of the leadership team lost faith in the inherent profitable growth potential of the McDonald's brand. They questioned the continued relevance of the brand.

The prevailing view was that significant profitable growth could not be achieved organically. A consultant advising top management stated that to be a growth stock, it was necessary to satisfy Wall Street's desire for 10% to 15 % annual growth.

So, instead of focusing on the organic growth of the McDonald's brand, McDonald's diverted its investment dollars to focus on growth by opening new stores and growth by acquisition of other brands. McDonald's seemed to adopt the concept, "BOB...Believe in Other Brands."

McDonald's acquired new brands through a series of acquisitions: Chipotle, Donato's, Pret-a-Manger, and Boston Market. This strategy only added to the depressed feelings among McDonald's franchisees.

In addition, new brand development efforts were given "green lights." There were investments in new concepts such as "McDonald's with a Diner Inside," and the development of a "3-in-1" McDonald's including not only a diner, but also a bakery and an ice-cream shop all under one roof. Whether it was the investment in new stores, acquisitions, or new concepts, the return on incremental investment was poor.

Flops, Fads, and Failures

McDonald's engaged in a frenzy of high-profile failures originally initiated to jump-start the brand. Here are a few of the more highly publicized ones:

- The high-priced Arch Deluxe was designed to bring adults into the franchise. Advertising featured kids turning up their noses at the mere mention of the Arch Deluxe, thereby sending a message that McDonald's was not for them. Alienating kids was certainly not a basis for profitable growth at McDonald's, the home of Ronald McDonald.

- The extraordinary Teeny Beanie Baby promotion had kids dragging parents in for the toys while tossing the food into trash bins. But, this had the unintended consequence of reinforcing the image of Happy Meals as a toy with food as an incidental attachment rather than as great-tasting food with a toy promotion attached.

- The unfortunate Campaign 55 confused people. It was nearly impossible to distinguish between the Campaign 55 "My Size Meal" and the still existing "Extra Value Meal" promotions.

- As profit pressure increased, McDonald's focused on cost management rather than on brand management. Costs were reduced by cutting product quality, no longer toasting the buns, modifying recipes, changing operations, and reducing staff in the stores. The belief was that the consumer would not notice—or, would not care. They did notice. They did care.

Love It or Leave It

At McDonald's, with a decline in food quality, poor service, inadequate product offerings, and order mistakes, it was not surprising that tactical, opportunistic monthly promotions became the dominant marketing focus. Happy Meals had become a promotion of a desirable toy, rather than a promotion for desirable food. This is not a way to build an enduring brand. Overemphasis on the deal rather than on the brand results in customers becoming deal loyal rather than brand loyal.

For brands to live forever, they must be loved forever. McDonald's leadership fell out of love with the McDonald's brand. And, consumers, franchisees, employees, and the financial community also fell out of love with the McDonald's brand.

The various tactics, strategies, and initiatives diverted attention from focusing on the number-one priority of revitalizing the McDonald's brand. Instead of being brand believers, McDonald's management became brand batterers. So it was no wonder that the beleaguered McDonald's brand posted its first-ever quarterly loss at the end of 2002.

The Times Are Changing

As if the loss of faith in the brand, and all these mistaken strategies were not enough, McDonald's ignored challenging developments in the marketing environment. Consumers were more informed, more skeptical, and more demanding. They were becoming more environmentally conscious and more health conscious. The issue of childhood obesity, which previously had only bubbled below the surface, became a major problem.[16] Issues such as these were subjects that few people at McDonald's even wanted to acknowledge, let alone discuss and prepare for. Instead of brand leadership, McDonald's resisted the developments in the changing world. This resistance to change is best captured in a *BusinessWeek* article in which Michael Quinlan, then chairman and CEO, said, "Do we have to change? No, we don't have to change. We have the most successful brand in the world."[17]

Ray Kroc's Vision

To further describe the context for the turnaround, it is worth briefly recapping Ray Kroc's story. It illustrates how truly unfortunate

---

[16] *The New York Times, The Wall Street Journal, The Economist, Advertising Age, BusinessWeek*, assorted articles, 1996-1998.

[17] Leonhardt, David, "McDonald's: Can It Regain Its Golden Touch?," *BusinessWeek*, March 9, 1998.

the state of affairs was in 2002. Ray Kroc was a visionary, a truly passionate dreamer. At an age when most people retire, Ray Kroc's vision was to create "a happy place." He envisioned the creation of a convenient, affordable, and pleasant way of eating quality food for a newly mobile, optimistic America. He democratized eating out.

Ray Kroc was relentless about making sure every customer feels special. He said that one of the greatest rewards is the satisfied smile on a customer's face.[18]

Unfortunately, the devolution from Ray Kroc's game-changing vision to a cheap-food-fast strategy generated customer scowls instead of smiles. Ray Kroc's vision was not just to be convenient and cheap. This would be a brand travesty. Ray knew that to deliver an exceptional McDonald's eating experience required more than being convenient and cheap. It required a dedication to quality, service, cleanliness (QSC), and a commitment to treating all customers with respect.

McDonald's leadership had become disconnected from the core values of the brand. The corporate memory turned dull. The connections to the founding principles were disregarded. Not surprisingly, customers became more and more dissatisfied.

Chain of Supply

While the front-of-the-restaurant experience was suffering, the McDonald's operational efficiency hummed along, focusing on cost efficiency rather than brand effectiveness.

McDonald's operations are second to none. There is really nothing like the McDonald's supply chain. How many times have you been to a restaurant where your waiter says the specials are no longer

---

[18] Kroc, Ray, with R. Anderson, *Grinding it Out*, Contemporary Books, 1977.

available? Now think about how you do not hear crew members at McDonald's telling you that Big Macs or fries are not available?

Think about the fact that each Extra Value Meal sandwich comes with a hamburger, chicken, or fish, condiments, a side item, and a napkin, not to mention a drink, a cup, and a straw. And that is just for the hamburger and chicken and fish sandwiches. Don't forget the breakfast sandwiches, Chicken McNuggets, various salads, a variety of desserts, other beverages, and so on. There are also a variety of packages and cups. The complexity of ensuring that the right inventory is in each of 30,000 restaurants, more than 50 million times a day in more than 100 countries, is an awesome challenge. For example, consider just these simple products such as the yogurt parfait or fries:

- **Yogurt parfait**—Plastic cup, plastic lid, spoon, napkin, granola packet, yogurt, and fruit. One size; seven items.
- **Fries**—Potatoes, salt, red fry box (three sizes), napkin, ketchup. Three sizes; five items.

Customers do not really consider this logistical miracle. Yet, it is all delivered at remarkable speed. It is all very efficient.

From an operational standpoint, all the food and accompanying items were in the restaurants. Sadly, what customers were too often experiencing in the front of the restaurant or at the drive-thru was an efficient yet off-putting experience of sloppy, inconsistent, and unfriendly service; inaccurate orders; and dirty outdated facilities. One customer described to me how he held his five-year-old son over the toilet rather than allow him to sit in a bathroom that was remarkably filthy.

This was the consumer, franchisee, and corporate environment when I joined McDonald's. It was not a pretty picture; McDonald's was not a happy place. But at least I was familiar with the causes for the challenges that lay ahead.

How McDonald's Declined

- Focus on growth by opening new restaurants
- Focus on growth through acquisition
- Incremental degradation of food, service, quality, and cleanliness
- Focus on cost management over brand management
- Focus on price and convenience alone

The Opening Salvo

For several years, Joan Kiddon and I worked with McDonald's on a brand strategy project. We advised on the development and articulation of a global brand promise led by Charlie Bell. I gave many presentations to groups of McDonald's employees around the world. We got to know the McDonald's brand and the McDonald's culture very well.

When Charlie Bell offered me the global CMO opportunity, he explained that McDonald's had never had a global CMO. Charlie pointed out that Paul Schrage, who retired in 1997, was really just a chief advertising officer. He was excellent at advertising judgment. But, according to Charlie, this new global CMO responsibility was greater than just advertising. It required a global redefinition of the brand's approach to marketing. Marketing would be about more than just advertising and tactical promotions. He said that McDonald's had decided to look outside for a leader with the right marketing perspective for the job. But, an outsider would need about a year to become familiar with the brand and cultural issues. He believed that with my McDonald's experience, I would be able to start immediately. And, he knew that I believed in the brand.

Mats Lederhausen, senior executive responsible for strategic planning, strongly reinforced Charlie's view that McDonald's needed a global CMO with a global marketing perspective. Both Mats and Charlie also convinced me that McDonald's would have to go outside to find such a person. My concern was whether the McDonald's culture would accept an outsider.

On August 31, 2002, I flew to Knoxville, Tennessee, to meet with then-CEO Jack Greenberg. Jack was under pressure to make McDonald's healthy again. He told me, "Eighty percent of our problems are in marketing. Marketing is broken. Marketing is not working." He said, "Your role is bigger than your title. You will be like a senior partner in a law firm. You will be a member of the executive leadership team."

What's Going On?

Before accepting the offer at McDonald's, I interviewed the top management. Among others, I spoke with members of the senior leadership team, including Matt Paull, Mats Lederhausen, Mike Roberts, Claire Brabowski, and Jim Skinner. There was amazing consistency in these conversations: The McDonald's business model is built on increased distribution. It was the "field of dreams" approach to growth—in other words, "build it and they will come."

They all agreed that the McDonald's brand was in trouble. They recognized that recent growth was attributable only to the opening of new restaurants, not increased visits to restaurants. They recognized that the brand image was suffering. Everyone seemed to agree that the business model was not working anymore, but no one had outlined what specifically was wrong and what had to be done.[19]

---

[19] Personal conversations, August 2002.

Joan and I discussed the McDonald's offer. We analyzed my discussions with the management team. We considered all the ramifications for our consulting practice that we had nurtured and grown over the past 20 years. What would this mean for our consulting business? How would we manage with one of us in Chicago and the other in Stamford, Connecticut? We concluded that this was a unique opportunity—an opportunity to put into practice our principles and to be accountable for results.

We saw the challenges. But we believed in the principles and process, and we knew that it could happen—we could help change and shape the trajectory of the brand.

Lack of Relevance

With the help of Joan Kiddon, we reviewed marketing research, read what we could find in the corporate archives, reviewed presentations and speeches, read McDonald's PR, met with a wide variety of people in different functions, and visited stores. I met with crew members, store managers, franchisees, and McDonald's executives. I talked to people who were familiar with the original brand vision, such as Fred Turner (Ray Kroc's right-hand man), Al Golin (Ray's PR advisor), David Green (previously chief marketing officer for International), Keith Reinhard (of DDB advertising), Cheryl Berman (of Leo Burnett advertising), Paul Schrage, Denis Hennequin, Dean Barrett, and others. It was clear from all of this information that McDonald's had lost its way. It was also clear that the brand had lost consumer relevance.

Loss of brand relevance was the key issue. The overarching challenge, then, was how to make the McDonald's brand relevant again. As a brand loses relevance, the customer base shrinks, and there is a decline in customer loyalty. At the same time, price sensitivity increases. Sales, market share, and profitability decline. The times had changed, and yet time stood still at McDonald's.

Many issues needed to be addressed:

- Outdated store designs
- Inconsistent advertising
- Overemphasis on deal promotions
- Declining product quality
- Lack of successful new products
- Poor service
- Insensitivity to increasing health consciousness
- Insufficient relevant choices
- Decline in Happy Meal sales
- Shrinking customer base
- Lack of organic growth
- Inadequate training
- Decreased franchisee confidence
- Reduced employee pride
- Inconsistent global brand focus

Successful brand revitalization would have to address all these issues. The first priority was a refocusing of the growth strategy. Jim Cantalupo redefined the growth goal from trying to grow by merely opening more stores to focusing on attracting more customers to our stores. Instead of the original plan of opening 1,300 new stores for 2003, Cantalupo reduced this to opening about 600 new stores.[20]

How would McDonald's meet its profitable growth objectives? Jim said, "We will grow by becoming better and not just bigger. We are going to do fewer things and do them better."[21] To be better, not

---

[20] Cohen, Deborah, "McDonald's to close 175 restaurants," November 8, 2002, www.rense.com.

[21] Garber, Amy Zuber, "McD Cooks Up New Strategy to Turn Around Chain," *Nation's Restaurant News*, April 21, 2003.

just bigger, McDonald's needed to move from being supply-driven to demand-driven. The mindset had to change from selling what we want to provide, to providing the brand experience customers want.

To restore McDonald's brand relevance, everything needed to be reexamined. Nothing was sacred. Everything communicates. Brand revitalization includes more than just advertising and promotion. It includes training, product development, store design, pricing, packaging, public relations, and human resources.

In late September 2002, in various conversations, I was told that McDonald's had lost focus on the brand. McDonald's had become so cost-driven that the focus was on finance rather than on brand-building. People were feeling that there was a lack of direction. McDonald's had lost its way.

McDonald's forgot Ray Kroc's (founder of McDonald's) view that we cannot just be a provider of convenient, low-cost food; we are an experience: We have entertainment value.

The McDonald's habit was to excite the owner-operators and try to address their concerns with new advertising at the biannual owner-operator conventions. Instead of focusing on the real challenges, the focus was on the advertising. In some cases, advertising created for the convention was rarely seen by consumers, if seen at all.

So, for example, when research showed that McDonald's service experience was a negative, rather than investing in improving the service, McDonald's launched a new advertising campaign, "We love to see you smile." Of course, consumers reacted negatively. Why should they smile, when the quality was cut, the service was inadequate, and the stores were not attractive?

Therefore, not surprisingly, among the first things I was asked to address was the need to develop new advertising. Creating new advertising is fun and makes for great conventions, but without addressing the real underlying problems, it does not produce great marketplace results.

New advertising without more fundamental brand experience improvements will not work. Merely launching new advertising is not a solution to a brand's ills.

For example, the Ford Motor Company launched an extensive advertising campaign touting its quality: "Quality is Job One." But, the product experience did not live up to the promise. After a 17-year investment in this message, Ford decided it was time to jettison this tagline.

Ford is now focused on improving quality. In June 2007, *The Wall Street Journal* reported that "Ford Motor Company made significant strides in a closely watched annual quality study in which each of the Dearborn, Michigan, auto maker's domestic brands came in above the industry average, helping the company close the gap with top Asian auto makers and distance itself from domestic counterparts."[22]

"The J.D. Power and Associates annual Initial Quality Study (IQS) released Wednesday, showed long-time leader Toyota Motor Corp. continuing to lose ground in the study, with its high-volume Toyota brand slipping behind Honda Motor Co. and barely outpacing Ford's Mercury brand. Ford was the most-awarded company on a vehicle-by-vehicle basis."[23]

However, to this day, Ford still suffers from a quality perception brand disadvantage. Now, that quality has improved, Ford can focus on marketing communications to close the gap in brand quality perceptions.

---

[22] *The Wall Street Journal*, "MarketWatch," June 6, 2007.
[23] Ibid.

Crisis of Complacency

Charlie Bell often reminded me that the McDonald's brand needed more insistence, consistency, and persistence. He would say that McDonald's fostered a culture of stagnation that breeds complacency. It is true that large companies sometimes suffer from a "complacency virus." Organizations like McDonald's have a tendency to stay with something that worked too long, assuming that all the benefits would continue to accrue without ever having to make a change. Doing things in the same old way, assuming that what worked once during the best of times would continue to work even though times had changed, would not help the brand stay relevant. It was just like Michael Quinlan said…why change? Complacency got in the way of generating passion and instilling pride.

Brand Re-Energization

Revitalizing a brand means not only must top management be the brand leaders, everyone in the organization must be a re-energized brand champion. So, to revitalize a brand, the major task is to re-create a brand culture aligned and inspired to deliver an exceptional brand experience to every customer, every time, everywhere.

My interviews with senior management and franchisees supported the idea that without a true commitment to the McDonald's brand promise, without the organizational change and accountability, McDonald's would not evolve. The turnaround at McDonald's would require what I call the *Three Cs*——clarity of direction, consistent implementation, and commitment from the top down throughout the organization.

The Three Cs of Turnaround

- Clarity of direction
- Consistent implementation
- Commitment from top down

Clarity of direction involves a clear statement of the brand purpose, promise, and goals. Consistent implementation requires that the organization must be aligned around that common focus and process. And commitment of the leadership means that people look up, not down, to determine whether they should also be committed to the new brand direction.

Passion and Pride

The sense of malaise and dispirit in the hallways of Oak Brook was overwhelming. Employee pride—a critical component of brand revitalization—had dissipated; people who were working on the brand did not really believe in the brand. Ray Kroc's vision of creating a happy place through serving people was lost. The sense of pride about working at McDonald's was gone: On Kroc Way and French Fry Alley, it was more funereal than fun-loving and friendly. People were experiencing a crisis of confidence.

Pride is not the same as satisfaction. Pride is bigger than just being satisfied with your job. Proud employees are engaged in their work: They are committed to helping inside and outside the company walls.[24]

Jon R. Katzenbach, a founder and senior partner of Katzenbach Partners, a national strategic and organizational consulting firm, had

---

[24] White, Erin, *The Wall Street Journal*, Theory & Practice (column), June 18, 2007.

this to say about employee pride: "Pride is more powerful than money. Employee pride is the powerful motivational force that compels individuals and companies to excel."[25]

Internal marketing is critical to brand accomplishment. To help revitalize employee pride, Rich Floersch, was hired from Kraft Foods as the new executive responsible for HR. His goal was to re-energize the employees through improved employee communications, and improved training. His leadership was a significant contributor to the brand turnaround.

When *Merriam-Webster's Collegiate Dictionary* announced that "McJob" would be added to its dictionary as a word describing "low paying and dead-end work," Jim Cantalupo reacted swiftly. In an open letter to Merriam-Webster, he argued that the term is "an inaccurate description of restaurant employment" and "a slap in the face to the 12 million men and women" who work in the restaurant industry. McDonald's e-mailed the letter to media organizations around the world. Cantalupo also wrote that "more than 1,000 of the men and women who own and operate McDonald's restaurants today got their start by serving customers behind the counter."[26] This kind of leadership passion and pride contributed to the rebuilding of employee pride. For successful brand revitalization, internal marketing must precede external marketing.

Cost Cutting Versus Brand Building

Brands get into trouble when cost management replaces brand management. Unfortunately, when brands get into trouble, the focus often turns to cutting costs rather than to brand revitalization. Cost managers become risk averse.

---

[25] Katzenbach, Jon, Katzenbach.com, January 1, 2003.
[26] Open letter from Jim Cantalupo to Merriam-Webster, Reuters, November 10, 2003.

Sears

Sears is an example of what happens when costs are cut to the degree that the brand becomes debased. Financier and Sears' Chairman, Eddie Lampert, whose hedge fund ESL Investments owns 49.6% of Sears, invested in computer systems for operations but did not invest in the stores and the in-store experience. The result is that in 2008, the stores are poorly stocked, dimly lit, and dirty. No wonder sales are down and profits have declined precipitously. And, as reported in May 2008, Sears Holdings posted a $56 million first-quarter loss.[27]

When a brand gets into trouble, enthusiasm and entrepreneurial spirit are often replaced by brand stubbornness. Standing still is for statues, not for brands. Brand lifelessness leads to brand losses, not to brand loyalty. The first step in brand revitalization is to face the facts of failure.

However, instead of trying to make each restaurant a more desirable destination, McDonald's focused on cost reduction rather than on brand building.

Our Leading Edge: Our Leaders

By the end of 2002, Jack Greenberg was gone. As mentioned previously, the retired former vice chairman and president Jim Cantalupo replaced Jack. Jim promoted Charlie Bell to become the new

---

[27] Kardos, Donna, "Sears Swings to a Loss as Weak Sales Hit Results," *The Wall Street Journal*, May 29, 2008; Jacobs, Karen and McCormick, Gerald E., "Sears Holdings Posts Unexpected Loss on Markdowns," Reuters, May 29, 2008; Fabrikant, Geraldine, "Sears Holdings Reports an Unexpected Loss," *The New York Times*, May 30, 2008; Birchall, Jonathan, "Sears Suffers Dismal Quarter of Poor Sales," *Financial Times*, May 30, 2008.

president and COO. Jim and Charlie's leadership focused on rebuilding the McDonald's brand with a renewed sense of urgency.

These were the two right people at the right time to lead the turnaround of the company. When Jim took the helm in January 2003, he refocused worldwide attention on not just being bigger but getting bigger by creating a better McDonald's experience. He stated that "Focus and discipline get the job done. That's what we're about. If we execute at a higher level, it is going to pay dividends on the top line."[28] We had to "right the ship."

Franchisees welcomed the renewed focus on the Golden Arches. "We have a lot of confidence and faith in the McDonald's brand," said Reggie Webb, a franchisee of 11 McDonald's restaurants in Southern California. "The best way to maximize on that future is to focus 100% on the McDonald's brand." Reggie was also the leader of the franchisee organization. He was among the original franchisee leaders supporting the new brand revitalization priorities.

Charlie Bell started working for McDonald's when he was 15. At 19, he was the youngest Australian store manager, eventually joining the Australia board of directors at 29 years old. Charlie held the positions of president of McDonald's Asia/Pacific, Middle East, and Africa Group, and president of McDonald's Europe before Jim chose him to be president and COO. He became my biggest supporter. His leadership was essential to the development of the McDonald's Brand Promise as well as the McDonald's Plan to Win.

It was an incredibly heady time. The doom-and-gloom scenario was transformed by Jim and Charlie's enthusiasm and unquenchable belief in the McDonald's brand. Together, they turned the sense of brand urgency into a galvanizing brand rallying cry of "being bigger by being better."

---

[28] Day, Sherri and Elliott, Stuart, *The New York Times*, April 8, 2003.

No matter what kind of brand you own, and no matter shape it is in, nothing is as positively contagious as a management team that passionately believes in the brand. As Jim Cantalupo expressed it, "Our competitors duplicate our standards, but they cannot duplicate the brand."[29]

The Plan to Win

Brand management is not a marketing concept; it is a business management concept. The McDonald's Plan to Win was built on this mindset. It could not be a regional initiative. It had to be global: consistent across geography, across time.

The Plan to Win is a business construct that is built on three pillars:

- **Brand direction**—Where do we want to be?
- **Freedom within a framework**—How do we plan to get there and what actions will we take?
- **Measurable milestones**—How will we measure performance?

Three Pillars of the Plan to Win

- Brand direction
- Freedom within a framework
- Measurable milestones

The Plan to Win is designed to guide brand thinking, the setting of priorities, and the development of a viable and feasible action plan.

---

[29] Buckley, Neil, "Burger Boss Needs to Flip the Fortunes of Big Mac," *The Financial Times*, December 17, 2002.

It is a business concept, crossing functions and geographies and organizational boundaries. It is the most powerful tool in a manager's toolbox. It affects every aspect of the business. The Plan to Win has four goals at its base:

- Attract more customers.
- Convince customers to purchase more often.
- Increase brand loyalty.
- Become more profitable.

In other words, more customers, more often, more brand loyalty, more profitable; these are the bottom-line goals for brand revitalization.

Four Goals of the Plan to Win

- More customers
- More often
- More brand loyalty
- More profitable

The Plan to Win is based on a disciplined thought process we call the *Eight Ps*. The Eight Ps of the Plan to Win represent eight critical areas for brand and business success: Purpose, Promise, People, Product, Place, Price, Promotion, and Performance.

Eight Ps of the Plan to Win

- Purpose
- Promise
- People
- Product

- Place
- Price
- Promotion
- Performance

Purpose and *Promise* define the brand direction. The brand purpose defines the overarching mission of the brand, and the brand promise is the contract with our customers. It is a promise that if you buy this brand, you will get this experience. A brand promise answers the question "what kind of brand experience do we wish to promise and deliver to every customer every time?"

The final P in the Plan to Win is *Performance*. Performance is the definition of the measurable milestones to assess our progress in brand revitalization.

The Five Action Ps

What are the actions we will take to achieve the measurable milestones? This brings us to the five action Ps: People, Product, Place, Price, and Promotion.

Delivering the brand promise is not determined by good intentions. It is accomplished by the actions we take. The five action Ps define how we plan to achieve the bottom-line goals of more customers, more often, more brand loyalty, and more profit. How we expect to deliver our promise across each of the five action Ps (people, product, place, price, and promotion) is articulated in the Plan to Win.

The details of the Plan to Win are discussed in Chapter 9, "Realizing Global Alignment: Creating a Plan to Win." The Plan to Win is a brand action blueprint. Adhering to the Plan to Win is critical for building brand revitalization.

Brand Power

Brand Power is another critical construct for brand managers. Our goal is to increase the value of a brand by increasing the power of the brand in the mind of the consumers.

A powerful brand is built on four elements:

- **Identity**—That particular set of ownable characteristics by which your brand is known

- **Familiarity**—Customer perception that they have enough knowledge about a brand to have an opinion about it
- **Specialness**—Perception of relevance and differentiation
- **Authority**—A reputation as a quality, leading, trustworthy source

To be a powerful brand, your brand goal must be to become the most familiar, highest quality, leading, most trustworthy source of a relevant and differentiated promised experience.

Brand Power

- Identity
- Familiarity
- Specialness
- Authority

Losing Brand Power

Familiarity with the brand identity is the easiest to achieve. And, increasing familiarity contributes to brand power. Studies have shown over the years that "share of voice" correlates with "share of mind."

The next step is not just to be familiar, but to be familiar with something special. Relevance and differentiation are the first to go when a brand is in trouble. Imitators or a better innovation can sap your brand's differentiation. Changing times can deflate brand relevance.

Authority takes the longest to build. And, once it declines, it is difficult to rebuild.

Familiarity is the last component of brand power to disintegrate. Once familiarity scores drop, the brand is on the oblivion train to commodity corner.

A Powerful Brand Is a Valuable Asset

Valuable brands do not just happen; we must make them happen. It takes a never-ending commitment to creating, nurturing, defending, and strengthening an enduring bond between a customer and a brand.

Summary

This was the state of affairs leading up to end of 2002. McDonald's was a brand in trouble. The brand had slipped and was mired in mediocrity. McDonald's leaders had fallen into the trap of believing that merely being bigger was enough rather than becoming bigger by being better. They believed that more of the same would continue to bring fortune and fame. They believed in a world that no longer existed and in customers who would never change. In 2002, McDonald's was a big brand, but it was tarnished. It was familiar, but it had lost relevance, differentiation, and authority. McDonald's was a brand ripe for revitalization.

2

The Six Rules of Revitalization

Whether your brand is IBM, Nissan, Apple, Harley-Davidson, Adidas, Gucci, Bayer aspirin, or McDonald's, a struggling brand can be revitalized. It is not easy, and it takes discipline. But it is well worth the effort.

Some people say that today's consumer is becoming less brand conscious. This is not true. Consumers want and seek out branded products and services. Even the so-called private label world is evolving from an emphasis on copycat brands sold on price alone, to exclusive store brands managed with differentiating value propositions. For example, Safeway, Wal-Mart, Target, IKEA, and Whole Foods embrace this approach to building consumer brand loyalty. As products and services, and life in general, become more complex, as markets become more fractionated, as choices proliferate, as time continues to be a precious commodity, and as customers continue to become more quality conscious, setting ever-higher quality expectations, brands will be more and more important to customers around the globe. Brands are one-think shopping. They facilitate and expedite decision-making.

Brand revitalization requires rigor and readiness to sacrifice what must be sacrificed. Deciding what not to do is as important as deciding what to do. This does not mean change for the sake of change. It does mean changing what is not working even if it is something that has been done for a long time and was a past contributor to brand success. It means a careful examination of resource allocation to assure that the limited money, time, and effort are allocated to those activities that are most likely to yield the desired brand and business performance outcomes.

In January 2003, one of Jim Cantalupo's first changes was to pull the plug on a \$1 billion technology project, code-named "Innovate," that Jack Greenberg had envisioned as a global digital network linking 30,000 McDonald's restaurants to headquarters and vendors.[1]

"We know we need to make changes," Mr. Cantalupo said soon after his return. But, he added, "We don't intend to throw capital at problems." Cantalupo won applause on Wall Street for slashing capital spending by 40%, putting the brakes on what many analysts regarded as runaway expansion of restaurants and by paying a significantly fatter dividend.[2]

Branding Is Not the Same As Advertising

Many corporate managers seem to believe that brand management is all about advertising and sales promotion. They believe that brand management applies only to consumer marketing but not business-to-business marketing. This is not true! A brand is a promise that if you buy a particular brand, you will get a particular experience. If you are making a promise to customers that your brand is a superior value providing a relevant and differentiated experience, then you are in brand management.

A Brand Versus a Product or Service

A brand is a distinctive identity promising superior value, delivering a relevant and differentiated experience, and indicating the source of that promise. A product or service is evidence of the truth of the brand's promise.

---

[1] "McDonald's ends project," *The New York Times*, January 3, 2003.
[2] *The Wall Street Journal*, Classroom Edition, April 2004.

What Is a Brand?

A brand is a distinctive identity promising superior value, delivering a relevant and differentiated experience, and indicating the source of that promise.

For example, when Procter and Gamble (P&G) revitalized Crest, P&G understood that Crest could be more than just a brand of fluoride toothpaste to prevent children's cavities. Today, Crest identifies the expanded promise of a lifetime of superior oral care including a wide variety of toothpaste, dental floss, mouthwash, tooth whiteners, and toothbrushes. Some say that extending brands like Crest beyond the original focus weakens the brands. Instead, a disciplined approach to brand extension can revitalize and strengthen a brand. Under the leadership of Jim Stengel, former CMO of P&G, a disciplined approach to brand extension has strengthened the Crest brand.

The Six Rules

In revitalizing a brand, there are six simple rules to follow. Just like the long-ago description of school—"reading, 'riting, and 'rithmetic"— these rules for brand revitalization all begin with the letter "R."

The Six Rules for Revitalization:

- **Rule #1**—Refocus the Organization
- **Rule #2**—Restore Brand Relevance
- **Rule #3**—Reinvent the Brand Experience
- **Rule #4**—Reinforce a Results Culture
- **Rule #5**—Rebuild Brand Trust
- **Rule #6**—Realize Global Alignment

Rule #1: Refocus the Organization

Rules require actions. In revitalizing the McDonald's brand, we not only had principles, we also had rules-based practices. Underlying the rules and the rules-based practices is the Plan to Win.

Refocusing the organization around common goals is the first step in creating a Plan to Win. What are our common goals? What is our common brand purpose?

To refocus the organization means moving from a provider mindset to a customer mindset. A provider mindset states: "How do we profitably sell what we know how to provide?" But a customer mindset means focusing on, "How do we profitably provide what we know our customers will want?"

It may sound trite, but it is true: The customer is the boss, and we must figure out the best way to please the boss. It is all about how we market to the boss. Or, as Phil Kotler and Gary Armstrong define marketing, it is all about *satisfying customer needs profitably*.[3]

Refocusing the Organization: The Practices

Refocusing the organization requires a total commitment to four actions:

- Explain brand purpose and goals
- Exercise financial discipline
- Enforce operational excellence
- Employ leadership marketing

We address each of these in Chapter 3, "Rule #1: Refocus the Organization."

---

[3] Kotler, Philip, and Armstrong, Gary, *Principles of Marketing*, 9th edition, NJ: Pearson/Prentice Hall, 2001.

Rule #2: Restore Brand Relevance

The second P in our Plan to Win focuses on ensuring the relevant differentiation of the brand promise. Where the first P—the brand purpose—provides an inspiring sense of corporate mission for the whole organization, the brand promise is an articulation of the relevant and differentiating experience that the brand will deliver to every customer, every time, everywhere so that we can make progress toward achieving the stated purpose.

How we define the brand promise is critical. Needs-based market segmentation is an important first step. It is also important to collect and synthesize the various opinions, views, and visions of people at all levels of the organization including the top management team.

Restoring Relevance: The Practices

Four things that must be accomplished to restore relevance:

- Develop a thorough knowledge of the market
- Adopt needs-based market segmentation
- Create customer insight
- Define the brand promise

Chapter 4, "Rule #2: Restore Brand Relevance," also discusses the use of the brand pyramid—the Arcature approach for helping to define the brand promise.

Rule #3: Reinvent the Brand Experience

A brand is a promise of an experience. To revitalize the brand, we need to revitalize the brand experience.

Reinventing the Brand Experience: The Practices

You cannot reinvent the brand experience without dedication to the following:

- Commit to an innovation program
- Perform renovation
- Focus on marketing
- Generate customer-perceived fair value
- Bring the total brand experience to life

The implementation of the Plan to Win should be examined from the standpoint of innovation, renovation, marketing, and customer-perceived fair value. The bottom-line goal is to enhance the total brand experience.

Some marketing experts say, "You cannot change people's minds." However, to revitalize a brand, you have to change people's minds—and you can.

Consumers do not know your brand strategy: They only know what you promise and how well you deliver the promise.

How do you bring the total brand experience to life? This is what the five action Ps are all about: assuring that we deliver what we promise. This is the focus of Chapter 5, "Rule #3: Reinvent the Brand Experience."

Rule #4: Reinforce a Results Culture

A former mayor of New York City, Ed Koch, always used to ask his constituents, "How am I doing?" A results culture is focused on evaluating progress toward achieving clearly defined measurable milestones. It is about knowing how we are doing.

People manage what management measures, recognizes, and rewards. Leadership needs to define how progress will be measured.

It is not enough to produce the right results. It is important to produce the right results the right way. The Plan to Win's performance measures assure that the right results are produced as a result of the right actions. It is important to produce the right business results.

It is also important that these results be based on a strong brand foundation.

Reinforcing a Results Culture: The Practices

The three critical actions are:

- Identify measurable milestones
- Implement recognition and rewards
- Initiate a balanced brand-business scorecard

Chapter 6, "Rule #4: Reinforce a Results Culture," describes the design of a balanced brand scorecard, which reinforces the importance of producing a proper balance of both business and brand results. It defines the measurable milestones.

Rule #5: Rebuild Brand Trust

A powerful brand is more than a trademark; it is a *trustmark*. Customers today are more knowledgeable, more demanding, and more value- and quality-conscious than ever before. At the same time, they are more skeptical, more questioning, and more uncertain. In this skeptical, demanding, uncertain world, trust is a must. When brand trust is in trouble, the brand will decline. Rule #5 focuses on rebuilding brand trust.

Rebuilding Trust: The Practices

The action for rebuilding trust is:

- Create and nurture internal and external commitment and behaviors

Are employees proud to say they work at your organization? Proud of the food? Proud of their job? Do they have confidence in the leadership? At the core of these questions is trust. Trust in the brand externally begins with trust in the brand internally: trust in the brand vision, trust in the brand quality, trust in the brand future, and trust in brand leadership.

When you create business targets that are missed year after year, credibility is lost—not just by the financial community, but also by other stakeholders. By the end of 2002, people were losing confidence in the McDonald's brand.

By first quarter 2003, McDonald's had missed its financial forecasts for five years running. Wall Street did not believe in McDonald's brand plans. Analysts questioned McDonald's on what the return was on the billions invested in opening new restaurants. But, not only Wall Street reviewed the forecasts with a wary eye: Employees did not believe the leadership. Internally, forecasts were greeted with disbelief. Why should people believe where we are going when they don't trust us? People merely waited for the next wave of cost cuts. Job survival had priority over brand success.

Trust can take years to build, but it can be lost overnight. As part of revitalizing a brand, trust needs to be rebuilt. This is discussed in Chapter 7, "Rule #5: Rebuild Brand Trust." Externally, as product and service quality declined, stores were not up-to-date, brand image deteriorated, health-consciousness increased, and consumer trust in the brand suffered.

Rule #6: Realize Global Alignment

The power of alignment is awesome. When a company unites around common goals, a powerful purpose, and a consistent promise, and has a Plan to Win, that company becomes unstoppable.

The inculcation into an organization of the Plan to Win creates an energizing movement for renewed success. Chapter 8, "Rule #6: Realize Global Alignment," focuses on the role of internal marketing and some of the concepts that help to align an organization and its outside partners and suppliers, and to revitalize a brand.

Realizing Global Alignment: The Practices

Creating a positive, global, revitalization mindset for the brand is a huge challenge. There are two actions for realizing global alignment:

- Execute the Plan to Win
- Establish Freedom Within a Framework

Establishing Freedom Within a Framework creates an organizing structure for thought and action on behalf of the brand that is both locally relevant while adhering to the global strictures. How does all this come together to create a coherent, consistent plan?

Realizing Global Alignment: Creating a Plan to Win

Creating and executing the Plan to Win is so fundamental that we devote an entire chapter—Chapter 9, "Realizing Global Alignment: Creating a Plan to Win"—to outlining how we put the eight Ps together and integrate these into the organization. The Plan to Win is a one-page document that reflects the principles of the Six Rules and the desired outcomes of the process steps. The commitment of top management to the Plan to Win is critical as well as the enthusiasm and dedication of the entire organization.

3

Rule #1: Refocus the Organization

People need a sense of purpose: They want to know that their work makes a difference. An organization must ask what is the shared sense of purpose, the common direction that will align us all and move us forward together toward a common destination. As Charlie Bell loved to remind us, paraphrasing the Beatle George Harrison, "We know from experience that...when you don't know where you are going, any road will lead you there."

The Plan to Win begins with defining the brand purpose. This means answering the question: *Where are we going?*

Refocusing the organization requires redefining the brand goals, realigning the organization behind a revitalized purpose and promise, and improving financial discipline, dedication to operational excellence, and leadership marketing.

Brand Purpose
Brand Purpose = Brand Goals and Brand Intent

Brand Purpose

Brand purpose is the first P in our Plan to Win. A brand purpose is the definition of the common brand goals and a compelling statement of the overarching brand intent or mission. It is not just a wish. It is based on informed judgment, not guesswork. It defines a clear sense of direction, an overarching goal for the organization and the brand. While defining where we want to go, the brand purpose must capture the desired spirit of the organization.

Brand Goals

In a brochure created for shareholders in October 2003, Jim Cantalupo described the organization's goals. He said,

> In 2003, McDonald's embarked on a new strategic course, reflecting a fundamental change in our approach to growing the business. Previously, we emphasized adding new restaurants. Today, our emphasis is on building sales at existing restaurants....
>
> Our near-term goals are to fortify the foundation of our business through operational excellence and leadership marketing and to lay the pipeline for long-term innovation. Attaining these goals will enable McDonald's to deliver consistent, reliable top-line and bottom-line growth and improve returns on invested capital."[1]

The new priorities became:

- Be bigger by being better.
- Instead of growing by building more stores, increase customer visits to our stores.
- Re-energize the brand.
- Improve profitability.

Brand Intent

Brand intent comes from those within the corporation. Consumers can tell you what they think they want now; they are not futurists. Consumers can complain, telling you what their problems are; they are excellent at this. But where you want to be, your brand intent, must come from the leadership.

The automobile entered the American scene around the turn of the century as an expensive toy for the rich. Henry Ford's intention

---

[1] "McDonald's Revitalization Plan," *McDonald's Corporation*, October 29, 2003.

was to produce an automobile that was reasonably priced, reliable, and efficient. In 1908, he introduced the Model T. It was the epitome of a no-frills utility vehicle—light, sturdy, plain, stripped of accessories, and selling for the low price of $825.

With the introduction of the Model T, a new era in personal transportation was launched. It was easy to operate, maintain, and handle on rough roads, immediately becoming a huge success. By 1918, half of all cars in America were Model Ts.[2]

Walt Disney's mission was to create a magical, happy place where children and parents could have fun together. With that intention, he focused on creating a high-quality, family-friendly, magical place... The Magic Kingdom. To lead change takes great personal commitment. Walt Disney once said, "It's no secret that we were sticking just about every nickel we had on the chance that people would really be interested in something totally new and unique in the field of entertainment." But, his passion prevailed. "All our dreams can come true, if we have the courage to pursue them."[3]

On its Web site, Whole Foods states "Whole Foods Company (WFC) opened its doors in Austin, Texas in 1980. Its mission was to be a grocery store featuring good, wholesome food; not a 'health food' store filled with pills and potions." Its motto is "Whole Foods, Whole People, Whole Planet."[4]

The mission of Google is to organize the world's information and make it universally accessible and useful.[5] Google's sense of purpose is to help make the world smarter.

As you can see, the brand purpose defines the brand goals and describes the organization's reason for being (intent). When revitalizing a brand, the organization needs a renewed sense of purpose, a renewed sense of direction. Jeffrey Abrahams says that a good mission

---

[2] The Henry Ford Museum, www.hfmgv.org.

[3] BrainyQuote, www.brainyquote.com.

[4] Whole Foods Web site, www.wholefoodsmarket.com, September 2007.

[5] Google Web site, www.google.com, September 2007.

statement must have content that can guide a company's decision-making process.[6]

The McDonald's Brand Purpose

To get everyone on the same page, we first need to define the page on which we want everyone to be.

Even before he was named president and COO of McDonald's in January 2003, Charlie Bell already had this one-page idea on his mind. He had generated a one-page plan while he was President of McDonald's Europe during 2002. He called it EuroMission.

Charlie believed that a similar one-page global plan to guide the global McDonald's revitalization should be immediately developed. Jack Greenberg endorsed Charlie's idea of a global plan and, in my new role as global CMO, Charlie asked me to begin working on its development. This work began in September 2002 and was completed by the end of the year. Out of this challenge, the McDonald's Plan to Win was born.

In January 2003, Jim Cantalupo and Charlie Bell announced the McDonald's Plan to Win revitalization plan. Instead of the growth priority being to build more stores, the new growth priority was to build customer visits to existing stores. The focus of the first year was "how do we get to great again?" The answer was "being bigger by being better."[7]

Getting everyone on the same page, the Plan to Win, produced immediate results. As Jim said in October 2003, "I am pleased with the momentum we are building. Our US business is ahead of the pace

---

[6] Abrahams, Jeffrey, "101 Mission Statements from Top Companies," reviewed in *The Wall Street Journal*, by Tofel, Richard. J., May 2, 2001.

[7] "McDonald's Revitalization Plan," *McDonald's Corporation*, October 29, 2003. In this brochure, McDonald's presented the Plan to Win to shareholders under the title of "McDonald's Revitalization Plan."

we set for ourselves at the beginning of the year. Nevertheless, we still have much to do to achieve enduring profitable growth around the world. Our revitalization plan is focused on reasserting McDonald's operational and marketing leadership, becoming more relevant to customers and managing our business for financial strength."[8] By the end of 2004, McDonald's was great again.

The previous McDonald's statement of intent was "To be the world's best QSR."[9] Many people interpreted this to mean that McDonald's mission was to be the ultimate "fast food" brand—fast and cheap.

Ray Kroc did not envision that McDonald's would be just another generic fast food joint. Ray Kroc never envisioned that McDonald's would be merely a convenient and cheap food distribution outlet. Ray Kroc believed that in addition to serving quality, affordable food with great service in a clean environment, the distinguishing experience of McDonald's was to be a happy place for employees and customers. Ray Kroc wanted customers to come back to McDonald's and look forward to regular visits. He wanted customers to find delicious, affordable food that they could obtain in an exceptionally clean and friendly environment. Ray Kroc was committed to treating the customer with respect. He believed that we needed to show that we really appreciate our customers' business. We should do things that will make customers know we care.[10]

To revitalize the McDonald's brand, we had to give the organization a renewed sense of purpose reflecting a revitalized Ray Kroc brand idea. This would be at the heart of becoming relevant again. We changed to a new customer-focused statement of brand purpose:

---

[8] "McDonald's Reports September and Third Quarter 2003 Sales," *AOL Business News*, www.prnewswire.com, October 7, 2003.

[9] QSR is the industry acronym for "Quick Service Restaurant."

[10] Kroc, Ray, *Forever Ray*, McDonald's, 2003.

It would be our brand mission of perfection; our Plan to Win would start with our specific statement of brand purpose.

Brand Purpose
To be our customers' favorite place and way to eat and drink.

The new articulation of the McDonald's brand intent was to become "Our customers' favorite place and way to eat and drink." Of course, we all knew that this was not how McDonald's was perceived at the time. But, our collective passion was that this is how we wanted McDonald's to be perceived. Jim and Charlie felt that for the first three years of the Plan to Win, we should focus on being our customers' favorite place to eat. The plan was that the phrase "and drink" would be added in the fourth year of the Plan to Win.

Going back to his days in Australia, Charlie invented the McCafé concept of delivering quality coffee at McDonald's. The current focus on new beverages, including improved coffee quality and choices at McDonald's is a direct outgrowth of Charlie's original vision. Charlie strongly believed that McDonald's could be and should be a beverage destination. He included a McCafé in the new McDonald's prototype restaurant near McDonald's headquarters, and he even built a McCafé in the lobby of the corporate headquarters to remind us on a daily basis that McDonald's can and should become our customers' favorite place and way to eat and drink.

Charlie believed strongly that we cannot waste our time debating short term versus long term. The long-term versus short-term debate is McDonald's terminal disease. He believed that if we don't do something effective now, there will be no long term.

We understood that it would be difficult to refocus the organization with a new brand purpose: a new business goal of being bigger by being better and a new sense of brand intent. We knew we needed to create a mental attitude inspiring everyone about what can be and what we could create together.

Having a tight disciplined focus with a set of priorities that crossed functions and geography provided shared beliefs and actions against which we could measure ourselves.

Customers

Refocusing the brand purpose meant changing the cultural mind-set from focusing on how to make customers want what we knew how to supply to focusing on how to satisfy what customers want. We would emphasize and turn into action Ray Kroc's passionate belief that we need to respect the customer.

Forest Mars, of Mars, Inc., makers of such brands as Mars Bar, Snickers, Pedigree dog food, Whiskas cat food, and Uncle Ben's rice, sincerely believed that "The consumer is our boss."[11]

Go into any Stew Leonard's store in New York or Connecticut and you will read and feel this, too. Ray Kroc believed the same thing. But over time, McDonald's had lost customer focus in the wave of huge restaurant openings.

McDonald's loss of customer connection was brought home to me in a variety of ways. The vast majority of McDonald's employees were not even around to learn why McDonald's was founded. Companies often develop a dull memory as they get farther away from the founding principles and principals. As corporations get bigger and bigger, it is not as easy to get the internal brand message out as before.

The implications of refocusing on the customer meant knowing customer needs, problems, behaviors, attitudes, and perceptions of the brand and its competitors. We will discuss how to do this in Chapter 4, "Rule #2: Restore Brand Relevance."

---

[11] *The Five Principles of Mars*, second edition, 1993.

Favorite

How could a restaurant like McDonald's be a favorite restaurant? Is this a reasonable goal?

"Morton's is my favorite restaurant." "Le Cirque is my favorite restaurant." These were the words of the vocal resisters to the word "favorite" in the new brand purpose. But McDonald's?

However, despite many people's skepticism, the concept of "favorite" stayed in the new purpose statement. Our goal was to be the favored brand within our competitive set of brands. We needed to refocus the organization on being a brand that our customers favored not just frequented. The majority of McDonald's most frequent customers did not favor eating at McDonald's. They just went there because it was so convenient and so cheap.

But valuable brands are brands that people prefer, not merely accept. This meant we had to become the brand that satisfies our customers' tastes and delights our customers' hearts at a superior value. The phrase we used time and again was, "We will no longer be satisfied if our customers just favor us with their frequency; we want them to frequent us because they favor us." Operational excellence and leadership marketing would make this happen.

We knew we were not there, but this was our goal. A statement of brand purpose needs to be forward-looking: It is a brand destination. It is an ambitious but possible dream.

Place and Way to Eat and Drink

It sounds so simple, but McDonald's did not really take notice that people's eating and beverage habits had changed. McDonald's failed to recognize that people's attitudes and behaviors were changing. To build brand favoritism, the McDonald's brand had to reflect the new understanding that people's behaviors were changing.

For example, take-out was growing and continues to grow. People were and are snacking more. People are eating at all times of the day.

They are more health conscious. They are more concerned about the food their children eat. They are more demanding of quality. They are more skeptical. They want more choices. They want more convenience.

The refocus on "place" meant revisiting the design of the restaurant. The old cookie-cutter approach of childish store designs was inappropriate for today's marketing realities. Not only did the restaurants need to be upgraded in general, but McDonald's had to adapt its restaurant designs to specifically improve relevance to local markets.

By emphasizing *place and way to eat*, we were committed to modernizing the restaurants and ensuring that these were clean, informal, and comfortable.

How, when, and where people eat varies by location, target audience, occasion, and need. So, for example, IKEA has cafeterias and cafés; service stations offer already-prepared foods; supermarkets have eating areas; and people eat on planes, in trains, in cars, at bars, and at desks as well as in dining rooms.

As the world became a 24/7 marketplace, McDonald's needed to extend its hours. Many restaurants agreed to stay open longer hours, and many of these offered 24-hour service.

We had to recognize the importance of take-away, snacking, and the increased importance of drive-thru. Drive-thru in the United States accounted for over 60% of sales.[12]

The new mission statement had an important effect on how McDonald's would be doing business in the future. It was not just a mere fluffy or generic statement. It articulated the future intent of the brand, highlighting the three critical components for the renewed focus: customer, favorite, place and way to eat.

---

[12] Minnik, Fred, "Expanding the Shrinking Drive-Thru," Digital Signage Association newsletter, March 2, 2006.

You cannot change your brand purpose and then do business as usual. To focus on being bigger by being better and to be our customers' favorite, we could not just compete on convenience and price alone. We had to promise and deliver a total brand experience that is perceived to be superior value. So, the next step in refocusing the organization was to redefine the value equation. We will discuss value again in more detail in Chapter 4.

The Value Equation

The value equation is simple:

The denominator of the value equation consists of the two brand budget basics of convenience and price. The numerator of the value equation is the promised experience that customers expect to get for their money and time.

$$\text{Value} = \frac{\text{Promised Experience}}{\text{Money and Time}}$$

The denominator of this value equation is important. Whether you call it "money and time" or "low price and convenience" or "affordable and fast"—what is in the denominator is the price to play, or as marketers like to say, "the greens' fees" or "the table stakes."

Some executives at McDonald's strongly believed that the generic concept of "affordable and convenient" was the essence of the brand. However, Jim Cantalupo, Charlie Bell, and Matt Paull, McDonald's CFO, recognized that focusing primarily on the denominator would not create enduring brand value. Denominator management leads to a low-priced, easy to use, generic, undifferentiated, commodity brand. As Matt regularly pointed out in presentations, focusing on convenience and price alone is a certain road to brand commoditization—a low-margin world.

There are brands with denominator positions, such as Wal-Mart promising low prices across an extraordinary assortment of products, from clothes to household goods to food to drugs. But, even Wal-Mart is vulnerable to competition from a brand such as Target that competes on more than price and convenience alone. Best Buy, Chipotle, Whole Foods, Safeway, Apple, IKEA, Toyota, and others recognize that there is more to the value equation than just the denominator.

To create enduring, profitable brand value, we need to do more than compete just on price and convenience. Ray Kroc knew the importance of the numerator as well as the denominator. He recognized that affordability and convenience were important. He also understood that the McDonald's brand advantage was more than just convenience and price. He taught that the McDonald's advantage was the respectful, friendly, fun experience that the customers receive for their time and money. Ray Kroc reminded everyone that McDonald's is a happy place—a place where anyone can afford to enjoy a happy eating experience.

McDonald's excessive focus on monthly tactical promotions and price deals may have built short-term sales, but these activities hurt customer-perceived brand value.

The corporate landscape is littered with marketers who focused on cutting costs by eliminating jobs, closing factories, and searching for synergies, but, at some point, there are no more people to eliminate, no more factories to close, no more synergies to synergize. Then what do you do?

Starving a brand as a strategy leads to brand anorexia. As Gregory Zuckerman and Kris Hudson wrote in *The Wall Street Journal* "Heard on the Street" column, "earnings gains that stem from cost cutting and more-efficient operations usually are less valuable than those from rising revenues because sales gains are considered more sustainable.[13]

---

[13] Zuckerman, G. and Hudson, K., "Heard on the Street," *The Wall Street Journal*, April 25, 2007.

As expected, there was resistance to change. Some believed that we should continue to do what we were doing but with greater effort. Of course, if the path you are on is a path of decline, greater effort on that path will only accelerate the decline. For a brand to be revitalized, a new path to the future needs to be defined and followed. And, strong leadership is a requirement, so that people will follow the leadership down the new road to the new destination.

In April 1993, when Lou Gerstner took the helm at IBM, the company was in dire straits. Although full of people who could build supercomputers, it was hemorrhaging money, losing more than $13 billion in two years. Its share of the mainframe market had plummeted by 50% and thousands of employees had left. IBM was truly in crisis, with the overhanging threat that investors would force a breakup of the venerable computer company.

Lou Gerstner was a strong leader. To make IBM a profitable company again, Gerstner shed assets, canceled products, cut prices, and fired staff. One of the notable changes was abandoning the OS computer operating system, and ceding market share to competitor Microsoft Corporation. Cutting the price of mainframes, which accounted for most of the profits, was another risky move, but "we had to do it to hang onto our customers. If we had failed, the company wouldn't have made it."[14]

But it was not all about cutting costs and prices. In Gary Hamel's recent book, *The Future of Management*, he discusses how Lou Gerstner made IBM more customer-centric and then Hamel draws lessons from Gerstner's and his executive team's approaches to challenging and changing the overall mindset and inevitably the culture.[15]

---

[14] Routson, Joyce, *Stanford GSB News*, "Gerstner Describes Bringing IBM Back to Health," www.gsb.stanford.edu/NEWS/headlines/vftt_gerstner.shtml, November 19, 2002.

[15] Hamel, Gary with Breen, Bill, *The Future of Management*, Boston, MA: Harvard Business Review Press, 2007, 216-229.

Lou Gerstner led IBM down a new path to a new revitalized future. When he left, IBM was once again in the black (the nearly $8 billion profit in 2001 marked the eighth straight year in the plus column) and back in the ring as the heavyweight to beat. Gerstner had convinced the highly intellectual, individualistic, $80 billion working culture at IBM to work as a team.

Jim Cantalupo's and Charlie Bell's leadership galvanized the organization. Their approach was based on a strong foundation of financial discipline, operational excellence, and leadership marketing.

Financial Discipline

In a brand revitalization plan, financial discipline is priority number one. Make money. Get back to profitability. Eliminate waste. Improve productivity. This is important. You need to earn the right to continue to grow.

When a brand gets into trouble, organizations often focus only on reducing costs rather than increasing brand value. The cost reduction approach shows up the fastest on the balance sheet. But without focusing on brand revitalization, eventually there are no costs left to cut. Al Dunlop cut back at Scott Paper and then sold the brand cadaver that was left to Kimberly-Clark.

Carlos Ghosn's approach at Nissan was different. He cut costs drastically, but he also believed in increasing brand value with new vehicles and new marketing. He was committed to revitalizing both business profitability as well as the brand.

Of course, eliminating waste and improving productivity is a continuing challenge. But, cost-cutting alone takes you only so far. You need plans, people, and actions that will deliver quality revenue growth.

Matt Paull, McDonald's CFO, was that kind of person. With his exceptional leadership, his department was a great supporter of the principle that at the core of sustainable profitable organic growth was the need to revitalize the McDonald's brand. Matt knew that McDonald's had to become more efficient in allocating its resources, improve productivity, and become more accountable in investing in new restaurants. But, he also knew that McDonald's needed to invest in updating existing restaurants, increase the quality of innovations, and revitalize the brand image.

Operational Excellence

Operational excellence means focusing on delighting customers so that an increasing percentage of customers looks forward to coming to McDonald's more often. Operational excellence meant improving product and service quality. The aim was to restore product quality to the original "gold standards." It meant revisiting and improving processes.

Operational excellence involves creating an efficient and effective balance between meeting customer expectations and at the same time minimizing waste.

Claire Brabowski was the leader responsible for operational excellence. She appreciated the challenges of restoring brand relevance as the basis for brand revitalization. She knew that cost management alone was not a formula for enduring profitable growth. As customer demands evolve and consumers require more choices, McDonald's needs to increase the variety of products on its menu. And, the need for real operational excellence increases.

Accurate forecasting is a McDonald's imperative. Forecasts are calculated using such items as store-specific historic product mix data; local, regional, and national factors; local events such as fairs, school holidays, and national promotions; store-specific information such as road closures; and a range of factors based on past performance, planned promotions such as sampling or special deals, and weather.

Operational excellence both decreases costs and improves customer satisfaction. Restaurants operate more efficiently, and customers receive the experience they expect. Improved efficiency allows McDonald's to control costs and deliver better value for customers.

Operational excellence includes more than just managing the supply chain. It includes ensuring consistent quality of the brand experience. Operational excellence is essential for any business. Cost management is a continuing challenge. It is always important to search for ways to increase productivity. But it is not enough to just be more efficient. It is important to be more effective. Leadership marketing gets people to the door. Operational excellence gets them to come back for more.

The goal is to be bigger by being better, and, to get better at being better. This requires better operations and better marketing.

Leadership Marketing

With strong financial discipline and a focus on operational excellence, the foundation is set for effective marketing. Leadership marketing is not defined by how big you are. Leadership is not determined by the size of the business. It is determined by the size of the ideas. It means innovating, not merely responding and reacting to competition.

The implication of focusing on financial discipline, operational excellence, and leadership marketing working hand-in-hand is to break down the silo mentality of many organizations. Everyone has a stake in the success of the Plan to Win.

The organizational responsibilities for realizing Jim's formula for enduring profitable growth were assigned as follows:

- **Financial discipline**—Matt Paull reporting to Jim Cantalupo.
- **Operational excellence**—Claire Brabowski reporting to Charlie Bell.
- **Leadership marketing**—Larry Light reporting to Charlie Bell.

Refocus the Organization: The Rules-Based Practices

- Explain brand purpose and goals
- Exercise financial discipline
- Enforce operational excellence
- Employ leadership marketing

The Do's and Don'ts of Refocusing the Organization

Do

- **Obtain top management commitment**—This kind of initiative will only work if the CEO, COO, CFO, and all the presidents are believers and are willing to implement. Everyone must be a believer.

- **Be specific**—Compose and articulate a simple, nongeneric purpose statement that can be easily communicated to everyone in the organization.

- **Create a core cross-functional team**—Be sensitive to the workings of the different departments within the organization. And, take advantage of their knowledge of the organization from their different perspectives.

- **Believe that nothing is sacred**—Be ready to change what needs to be changed, including the sacred cows such as a business model or financial targets.

- **Recognize what has failed**—Do not hide from or misstate the truth. Your people deserve to know what is not working, why, and how they can rectify any mistakes. Learn from failure.

- **Know the business you are in**—Are you in the restaurant business, the fast food business, or the business of delivering an exceptional eating experience?

Don't

- **Don't be vague**—Being generic means you really do not have a clear idea about where you want to be and what you want to do.

- **Don't ask your customers what your vision should be**—The purpose of your brand comes from those inside the company. If the person in the focus group is such a prescient seer that he or she knows where you should be headed over the next couple of years, hire him or her.

- **Don't reject your heritage**—Your business was built on something good. You can be contemporary and still leverage your past. Old can be new again.

- **Don't extrapolate the present**—This is the future world; it may be different from where you are today. This is not about defending the status quo but about having the foresight to articulate what you want to be.

- **Don't practice corporate isolationism**—Top managers in regions other than where HQ resides have contributions to make. Open the doors to your geographies. Be collaborative instead of combative.

4

Rule #2: Restore Brand Relevance

Remaining relevant in a changing world is critical to a brand's health. Relevance is a key driver of purchase intent. But increasingly trust is becoming critical as a driver of purchase intent. Of course, it is important to be different. It is important to be relevant. But just differentiation and relevance without trust is a formula for failure.

Trust is a foundational factor on which effective brand relevance and differentiation can be sustainable. We discuss trust in Chapter 7, "Rule #5: Rebuild Brand Trust." For now, we focus on the principle and the practices necessary to bring about the restoration of relevance.

When brands lose relevance, customers believe that a company does not understand them anymore. They begin to think that the company is no longer interested in supplying them with what they want, but rather that the company wants them to buy what it is prepared to supply.

To restore brand relevance, we must:

1. Begin with developing a thorough knowledge of the marketplace.
2. Conduct and have a true understanding of market segmentation. Understanding market segmentation is fundamental to brand revitalization.
3. Create insight into customers.
4. Prioritize the market segments.
5. Using knowledge and insights, we must define the promise of the brand to appeal to the prioritized market segments.

Jim Cantalupo emphasized the necessity of changing to become relevant for McDonald's customers. He said: "The world has changed. Our customers have changed. We have to change, too."[1]

Thorough Knowledge of the Marketplace

As Joan and I learned, there is a lot of unused information in a big company like McDonald's. All sorts of information is generated, collected, codified, and filed. Most of this information is filed away. Sometime it is read and then filed away. Country-specific information tends to stay in the country even if it has ramifications globally.

Our advice is to find all the information you can. Then read it. Someone must have thought there was value to generating a particular report or writing a particular white paper or research study. With the Internet and selected services such as LexisNexis, information on just about any topic is available. Be aware of what is going on—in your category, in your country, across geography, in the art world, in the cultural landscape, and so on.[2]

Before we created the McDonald's segmentation, we asked to see what segmentation work had been conducted in the past. We learned that more than 100 studies that could be called segmentation studies had been conducted since 1988. These studies contained great information.

If you want to be a learning organization, you have to learn who you are, what you know, what the world is, and what it possibly will be like.

---

[1] "Did Somebody Say a Loss," *The Economist*, April 12, 2003.

[2] When our consulting firm begins a project, we ask for information. The list of the kinds of information we ask for is in Chapter 9, "Realizing Global Alignment: Creating a Plan to Win," in the section, "Step 1: Brand Direction."

Understanding the Market Segmentation

A *market segment* is a definable group of people or organizations that share common needs in a common context. "Need" is the critical concept.

What is not a market segment? A market segment is not a product category. It is not geography. There is no such thing as the French market, the Japanese market, or the Italian market. Geographies are where market segments exist. Geographies are how you organize to deliver the brand promise to the prioritized market segments.

Product categories are not market segments. So, for example, there is no lip-gloss market; there is no mascara market. But there is a market for attractiveness, for youthfulness, for status, and for elegance.

There is no such thing as the automotive market. Nor is there such a thing as the soft drink market or the pet food market or the hamburger market. Products are what we sell to the market; they do not define the market.

If you want a vehicle for driving your children to soccer practice and saxophone lessons, you might consider a Chrysler minivan, a Volvo wagon, or a Toyota SUV. These would all satisfy the same need. Yet, the automotive industry places each of these types of vehicle in a different category because they tend to look at product classifications rather than needs-based market segmentation.

A market segment is a want. If there is no want, there is no market. If there is a global want, there is a global market. If there is a growing want, there is a growing market. If some people in France and some people in Australia share the same want, then they are in the same market. It just happens that they live in different places. If the want is incorrectly defined, the market segment is incorrectly defined.

The role of marketing is the process of profitably providing branded products and services to satisfy customer wants at superior customer-perceived value compared to competitive alternatives. The goal is to attract customers and to increase their brand loyalty.

Sometimes the best way to persuade people is to convince them that you offer a solution to one or more of their leading problems. When a brand can solve one or more of a customer's leading problems, it is providing the desired benefits. People tend to be risk-averse. The avoidance of pain or the need to solve a problem is a stronger motivator than the attainment of pleasure. That is, people will usually pay more to avoid an unpleasant consequence than to attain a pleasant one. The problem-solution approach is a practical, flexible, and effective approach to the challenge faced by marketers, designers, and R&D teams when it comes to product/service renovation and innovation.

Dyson understood that many consumers had bothersome problems with their vacuum cleaners. They did not like cleaning the bags. And, they became frustrated trying to find the right bag for their specific machine. Dyson came up with a bagless vacuum cleaner. Then, Dyson promised the added benefit of maintenance of superior suction power, a perceived problem with previous conventional vacuums.

Diet Coke satisfied the want for a diet cola that tasted great.

Sometimes a want can be satisfied with a small renovation such as the Chrysler minivan "fourth" door because people were becoming frustrated with second row access from only one side of the vehicle.

Satisfying customer desires is the key differentiator between marketing and selling. Selling is about convincing customers to buy what we know how to provide. Marketing is about providing what we know customers want or will want. Superior understanding of consumer needs provides the basis for outstanding competitive advantage.

Market Segmentation

The process of market segmentation is about dividing people into different "markets" that share common needs and are differentiated from people in other segments who share different needs.

Those who look at market segmentation as just another research tool miss its real strategic value. The information provided by insightful market segmentation helps direct brand policy, marketing strategies, and resource allocations. It allows you to identify priority areas for innovation. It helps define your competitive set sometimes in ways that are different from what you currently believe. Effective market segmentation drives business strategy, not just brand strategy.

We no longer live in a world where mass marketing works. We no longer live in a world where mass marketing to masses of consumers with a mass message delivered through mass media makes money. In fact, mass marketing as we knew it is dead. In 2004, the cover story of *BusinessWeek* was "The Vanishing Mass Market."

As *BusinessWeek* said, our country has "atomized into countless market segments defined not just by demography but by increasingly nuanced and insistent product preferences." They said that it is a whole new world.[3]

Mass marketers lack focus. There is no central point of interest. Mass marketing tries to appeal to everyone, but the result is an average message that everyone likes a little and nobody likes a lot. Market segmentation helps to identify the different groups of people, their needs, and the circumstances in which they use the brands. A former client of ours at Mars liked to say that effective market segmentation provided *FEDA*, a *focused enduring differential advantage*.

The discipline that we use for defining the market segmentation is based on a principle originally described by Rudyard Kipling, which he called his "six little friends": what, who, why, how, when, and where. In marketing, what people want is a function of who they are, why they use, and the context in which they use (how, when, and where they use).

---

[3] Branco, Anthony, "The Vanishing Mass Market," *BusinessWeek*, July 12, 2004.

Since our approach is to first understand people's needs, we first ask *why* the customer uses: What are the wants underlying usage? What are the problems with what the customer currently uses? Then, we look at *who* are the people who have these needs. This is called *profiling* the segmentation. The next step is to define the *context* (*how, when, and where*) in which different needs exist.

PRODUCT Classification

Journals and market research professionals discuss many different ways to segment. For example, some marketers use product categories as the basis for market segmentation. This is easy and inexpensive. You just divide up the category by the types of products available.

We see this in many categories. For example, in the automotive business, you now have divisions such as midsize, luxury, SUV, and so on. Today, the product segment refinements in the automotive industry border on bewildering definitions such as luxury, mid-luxury, near-luxury sedan, or premium.

A recent story in *Automotive News* describes the key segments identified by Ford in its desire to have a global platform. Putting aside the issue of reducing manufacturing complexities, the article demonstrates the problems that a company can fall into when it sticks with a product segmentation that is actually product classification. With no needs attached, how do you distinguish between a B-car, a C-car, a CD-car, a CD-crossover, a compact, a midsized, and a rear-wheel-drive car?[4]

Product segmentation is a manufacturer's view of the market: assorting and assigning market segment definitions based on what products are made based on product characteristics. So, for one

---

[4] Wilson, A., "One Ford, Many Key Segments," *Automotive News*, April 30, 2007.

appliance maker, the segmentation was "hot," "cold," and "wet." No consumer ever asks for a hot appliance. They want a stove or conventional oven or microwave or toaster oven or grill that can address such needs as warming, defrosting, reheating, cooking, baking, grilling, and sautéing, and doing these tasks quickly, slowly, overnight, or in real time. And, where do you place a dishwasher that both wets (washes) and dries (hot) your dishware and cutlery?

McDonald's held to the idea that since it was a big brand, it must appeal to everyone for every reason. There were some who resisted the McDonald's needs-based segmentation saying that McDonald's was a "burgers and fries for everyone" brand.

This is wrong. It is product categorization, not needs-based segmentation. And brands cannot appeal to every person for every occasion. By trying to appeal to an undefined mass market, the result is inevitably a mass message of mediocrity.

WHY Segmentation

WHY *segmentation* focuses on specific needs, functional and emotional. This is the basis for meaningful market segmentation. Needs-based segmentation begins by identifying people or organizations that share common needs and are different from those who share different needs.

It focuses on why people do what they do. WHY segmentation helps drive product and service design, R&D, positioning, pricing, and sales and marketing. A WHY segmentation for suntan lotion could look like this:

- Those who just want a deep, dark tan
- Those who want to tan naturally while actively participating in outdoor activities
- Those who are concerned about getting dry, flaky skin from too much sun
- Those who are worried about skin cancer and want maximum protection

We can define needs-based market segments in terms of functional needs or emotional needs or a combination both types of needs.

But, WHY segmentation alone does not tell us who has the needs; it just tells us the different needs groups that exist. It does not tell us in what contexts these needs occur. This brings us to the Who × Context dimensions of market segmentation. Having defined the needs segments, the next step is to profile these needs: Who has the needs in what contexts?

WHO Segmentation

WHO segmentation helps us to profile the needs segments in terms of demographics, lifestyles, behaviors, or values. This is important. It is also the most fun because it provides a deeper understanding of people. Advertising agencies love WHO segmentation. It is helpful for creating so-called lifestyle-advertising campaigns. Understanding the WHO of the brand segmentation helps to build a brand connection with the customer.

However, without a thorough understanding of customer needs, it is difficult to implement and operationalize brand development strategies. The Gap thought that "age segmentation" alone, would be the way to boost profitability. So they developed the Forth & Towne retail stores with clothing designed for the over-30-year-old female. When the chain was closed, the press described a misunderstanding of the shopping habits of the 35-year-old woman and a whole slew of other reasons why the Forth & Towne stores failed.[5]

What these reports neglected to say was that women over 30 years old do not all have the same needs, or the same attitudes. "Women over 30" is not a market. What was the need that Forth & Towne intended to satisfy better than alternatives? This was not clear.

---

[5] Barbaro, Michael, "Gap Closing Chain Aimed at Over-30s," *The New York Times*, February 27, 2007.

WHO segmentation alone does not focus only on consumer psyches. It does help us to profile the needs segments in terms of the distinguishing characteristics of the people who have the identified needs.

Profiling the people associated with the identified needs segments helps us not only to understand the needs better, but also helps us to develop our marketing plans.

CONTEXT Segmentation

CONTEXT segmentation is based on the fact that people have different needs in different contexts. As the situations change, sometimes so do the benefits desired by the customer. For example, you might want one type of beer when you are at a ball game, and another type of beer when you are dining with a client, and another type of beer when you are at home hanging out with some friends while watching TV.

It is helpful to understand how, when, and where a consumer has a particular need. Again, focusing on context alone is not enough: It must be associated with specific needs and specific people who have these needs to grasp the full picture of the market.

Think about beverages. Occasions could be segmented by context:

- Start the day
- Between meals
- With meals (breakfast? lunch? dinner?)
- Alone
- With kids
- With friends
- With business associates
- In the evening

But, this does not provide insight into what needs people have at these different occasions. And, it does not tell us who has these needs.

The primary determinant of market segmentation is first driven by needs. Our brand goal is to profitably promise and deliver the superior satisfaction of specific customer needs at superior value.

That is why we begin with needs-based segments. Then these are profiled in terms of who and context (how, when, and where).

Needs-Based Segmentation Profiles

What do you do now? We put all this information together to create a multidimensional view of the market: What people buy and use is a function of why they need it × who they are × context of use (how, when, where).

For example, needs-based market segmentation for the original Starbucks concept might look something like this. Four basic needs (WHY): I am thirsty, I need a lift, I need to take a pause, I want to enjoy a small luxury.

- **Four key coffee occasions (CONTEXT)**—Emergency, at home, coffee break, and café society.
- **Four people segments (WHO)**—Day-timers, night crawlers, new-agers, and connoisseurs

Starbucks chose originally to focus on the "small luxury" need segment. Profiling this need led to the concept Starbuck described as the "third place"—a place away from home and work appealing to those connoisseurs who want the "small luxury" of a premium quality "café society" experience.

Prioritizing the Markets

These three dimensions (WHY × WHO × CONTEXT) define the market. As we described in the example of a vehicle for driving children to events, the customer, not the marketer, defines the market. If the brand is the source of the promised experience made to the customer, then it is the customer's perspective of the market that matters. Customers tell us what alternatives they consider when they have a specific need in a specific context.

For example, much of the business press sees McDonald's as a hamburger restaurant. They report market share and brand performance comparing McDonald's to the other major hamburger brands. And many McDonald's managers agreed. But this is misleading. McDonald's satisfies a variety of needs for a variety of people in a variety of contexts. Children have different needs from teens and young adults and parents. The needs are different at breakfast, snack, lunch, and late night. McDonald's competition is different at breakfast compared to lunch. So, the competitive set is different for each of these WHYs × WHOs × CONTEXTs.

If you are a business traveler about to board a flight home, you may need a meal to eat on the plane. The airport food court creates the competitive set. Your needs may be the ease of carrying the meal one-handed and/or the tidiness of eating the meal on a cramped tray-table. These needs would be different from the needs you would have if you were at a booth in the same restaurant brand in the strip mall near your home with a friend.

Proper market segmentation is fundamental to modern marketing. Superior understanding of customers, their needs, who they are, and in what context they have these needs, provides the basis for outstanding competitive strategic advantage.

However, any research tool is as much an art as a science. Market segmentation is not the absolute answer. It cannot reveal what you must do tomorrow. Market segmentation provides the landscape on which you creatively and intuitively understand where the best current and prospective territories are for your brand.

To find competitive advantage in our fast-paced, changing world, we must have the clearest understanding of our customers from all angles: What they buy as a function of why they buy, who they are, and how, when, and where they use what they buy.

Snickers

The revitalization of the Snickers candy bar in 1993 hinged on the observation that a big, intrusive hunger gets in the way of completing a task (WHY). The target audience (WHO) was young adults. The context (HOW, WHEN, WHERE) was eating a slice of pizza, a large muffin, or a big cookie to satisfy this big hunger. This hunger was particularly intrusive in everyday situations at work, while studying, late at night, and so on. Previously, Snickers was marketed merely as a great-tasting chocolate-covered bar filled with peanuts, caramel, and nougat. Astute observation of consumers and a keen understanding of consumer needs and snacking changed the brand's trajectory.

The New York Times reported in March 2007, that for 44 years the Wal-Mart mantra had been "Low prices, always." Then Wal-Mart adopted a new approach based on market segmentation. Wal-Mart segmented its customer groups with different wants:

- **Brand aspirants**—People with low incomes who are obsessed with (need to own) brand names.
- **Price-sensitive affluents**—Wealthier shoppers who love a good deal (want to feel smart).
- **Value-priced shoppers**—People who like low prices and cannot afford much more (need to stay on a tight budget).

According to the story, "From now on all product decisions will be organized around the three groups." Wal-Mart, recognizing the differences and the common characteristic of the love for the deal, created "five power product categories with these three groups of customers in mind: food, entertainment, apparel, home goods, and pharmacy."[6] Big brands deal with fundamental human truths. Generating a global market segmentation depends on identifying universal human truths

---

[6] Barbaro, Michael, "It's Not Only About Price at Wal-Mart," *The New York Times*, March 2, 2007.

that exist around the world regardless of geography, time, or space. The satisfaction of a "big hunger" for Snickers is a universal truth.

Looking for the "best deal" is a universal truth. Coca-Cola's satisfaction of "refreshment" is a universal truth. And, big brands like McDonald's also focus on fundamental human truths. These truths are the shared common denominators that remain stable over time.

While a global brand shares common, universal human truths, the interpretation of these truths must be adapted to relevant local market conditions.

Customer Insight

Interpreting your information and your market segmentation is more than reading—it is an art form. It is not sufficient to take the print-out with the statistical data and say "Voila!"

The same raw data can and should be analyzed a variety of ways using many statistical approaches. Look into the data not just at it. But, analyses alone do not reveal truth. To the information, we need to add insight.

Insight is such an overused, misunderstood, and misappropriated term in marketing and marketing research departments. Insight is an underlying human truth about how the target users really think, feel, or act: It helps you to identify unarticulated wants.

To be insightful, you must be open to everything, and you must use everything. You must not only see the data, but also understand what is behind the data. You must apply imaginative escape with disciplined thinking. You must be able to make connections among things, ideas, and visuals that before were unconnected. Think of insight as informed intuition where intuition is the ability to see into the heart of things—seeing beyond appearances. Insight requires sensing, studying, experiencing, and ingesting the present.

You will need to look at your information and your statistical output with a creative eye, not just a mathematical brain. Is there anything surprising? Is there anything that gives you an "aha" moment?

Do your best to make the information meaningful. I wish there were a process for generating customer insight. There is not. It is part of the process, but to do it you need a certain kind of mindset.

Synthesis Versus Analysis

Here is where a new mindset is necessary. In marketing, synthesis will triumph over analysis. Business schools typically teach that through superior analysis, a great creative insight will be revealed leading to a great innovation. This is unfortunate. Analysis leads to an understanding of *where we are now and how we got here*. Analysis does not lead to understanding where we should be going. The analytic, backward-looking, approach of inspection, retrospection, and dissection cannot help us create our future. Creative breakthroughs are not born out of detailed analysis; they are born out of creative synthesis.

Relying only on detailed analysis leads to idea paralysis. Analysis is about taking things apart. Synthesis is about creatively integrating, rearranging, and reordering familiar elements in unfamiliar ways.

In November 2003, an article in *Harvard Business Review* observed that "true innovation and strategic value are going to be found more and more in the 'synthesizers'—the people who draw together stuff from multiple fields and use that to create an understanding of what the company should do."[7]

It is important to identify trends. They are ideas and concepts that happen around us and influence the way and manner in which we behave. Trends are valuable because they inform us about what is presently happening in the world around us. But trends are not insights into where we should be going. Trend analyzers try to forecast the future. Creative synthesizers look for ways to create the

---

[7] Anderson, Chris, "Finding Ideas," *Harvard Business Review*, November 2003, 18-19. Also see Gardner, Howard, *The Five Minds for the Future*, Boston: Harvard Business Review Press, 2007. Howard Gardner provides a clear understanding of the differences and overlaps of synthesizers and creative thinkers.

future. To create the future, we need synthesis, and for synthesis we need synthesizers.

Synthesizers are different people. They think differently. They like ambiguity, analogy, and paradox. They are curious. They make the strange familiar and the familiar strange. Synthesis takes crafts people, artists, and physical and social scientists who see patterns that we overlook or just cannot see, and who can form foresight from fragments of evidence and seemingly unconnected information. Synthesis is essential to the new mindset for the future. Synthesizers will triumph over analyzers.

Prioritize, Prioritize

No brand, no matter how big can address every opportunity effectively. The imperative is to prioritize. And it defeats the purpose of focus to set out to address all the identified market segments. You must put a stake in the ground somewhere. Where do you draw the brand's territorial boundaries?

So, the next step is to prioritize the market segmentation. This is a difficult decision for many executives. It is much easier to say "Yes" to the high-priority segments. But, it is often difficult to say "No" to the low-priority segments. You hear executives say: "We cannot eliminate anybody." "We want to appeal to everybody." "Why are we focusing on young adults? What about empty nesters or seniors?" But, prioritization of the market segmentation is important.

Prioritization does not mean that a brand should focus on only one segment. It also does not mean that a brand can treat every segment equally. Prioritization helps us to decide which segments to focus on.

It requires an understanding not only of our strengths and weaknesses but also of trends and future opportunities. Of course, it also requires consideration of the available resources.

Research techniques alone should not be the only way you select markets. The segments need to be set against the backdrop of your foresight into the future. Think of the possibilities within each segment. Think about what can be as well as what already exists. The market segmentation opportunities you uncover provide direction for stimulating vibrant ideas for growth.

How do you prioritize the market segmentation? Evaluate each segment in terms of both the relative competitive advantage and segment relative opportunity attractiveness.

Here is one tool that we recommend. A two-dimensional analysis like the one in Figure 4.1 helps to prioritize the segmentation. Segments E and F are high-priority opportunities. Segment B may be a great opportunity; however, we need to build organizational competence and develop competitive advantages to compete in this segment. We have a competitive advantage in appealing to segment C, but this is a lower-priority opportunity for profitable growth. Segments A and D are best ignored. We have little competitive advantage, and they represent low profitable growth opportunities.

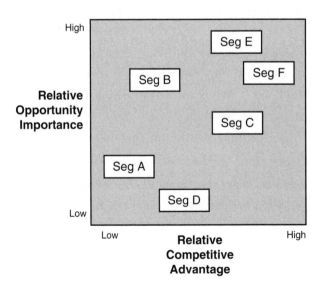

Figure 4.1   Market segment prioritization

Leadership Marketing

Leadership means leading the way to the future. Marketers need to lead the way to a new brand destination. McDonald's knew that internal marketing would be as important as external marketing. We rebranded the role of marketing at McDonald's, calling it *leadership marketing*. As we mentioned in Chapter 3, "Rule #1: Refocus the Organization," leadership marketing is a critical path to refocusing the organization.

The word "leadership" came first because exhibiting leadership is so important to brand revitalization. Leading means rejecting outdated, outmoded ideas of the past. Leadership means providing the strength to jettison marketing practices and mindsets that forced the brand into brand-damaging marketing directions.

Here is an example of the way we exercised leadership marketing to provide brand relevance. A huge, mega-brand like McDonald's cannot follow the accepted principle that works so well for niche brands: Find a single consumer niche that you can dominate.

So, what is the solution? The choice between mass marketing and niche marketing is a false dilemma. The answer is multisegment marketing. As controversial as it was when we adopted this multisegment strategy at McDonald's in 2003, the results demonstrate that this approach is correct. Other brands have adopted similar approaches; for example, Best Buy segments by five initial core customer groups:

- Early technology adopters
- Suburban mothers
- Small businesses
- Affluent professionals
- Family fathers

In an article in the *Financial Times*, the reporter discusses how Best Buy is beginning to focus on two or three of these five groups.[8]

McDonald's Segmentation

While there were many potential market segmentation opportunities, prioritization was critical. McDonald's product and service focus was to provide convenient, affordable, quality food in a clean and friendly environment. McDonald's referred to this operations strategy as QSCV—quality, service, cleanliness, value. But as a brand strategy, McDonald's adopted multisegment, multidimensional marketing.

McDonald's prioritized its marketing resources to focus on three key segments with different needs:[9]

- Great tasting food and fun for kids
- Healthful eating for young adult moms
- Satisfying food for young adult males

Kids are very important to McDonald's. They are an important part of the brand heritage. Moms are important because they play a key role in influencing the family's eating habits. And young adults are important because they are both a growth opportunity and an important part of the new change in brand attitude.

These three key segments identified the "why × who." McDonald's also identified four priority contexts: lunch, breakfast, late hours, and snacking.

McDonald's changed from an unfocused mass marketing to a multifocused brand, focusing on specific market segments with specific marketing messages and specific products.

---

[8] Birchall, Jonathan, "Best Buy Plots its Global Strategy," *Financial Times*, May 13, 2008.

[9] This concept was shared publicly on various occasions during 2004; for example, Advertising Age, June 2004 and Association of National Advertisers, October 2004.

What Is the Brand Promise?

A brand is not a single word. Some marketing experts say that we should reduce a brand to a single word and aim to own that word in a customer's mind. This is simple to say. But it is simplistic marketing. A brand is an idea—a multidimensional, multilayered, multifaceted idea. Simplifying a brand to a single word ignores the complexities of a brand and dilutes its appeal. Big brands like McDonald's are not unidimensional.

Now that we have identified the priority markets for our brand, what is the differentiating brand idea? What is the brand experience we want to promise and deliver to every customer every time? How we articulate that promised experience depends on five specific components: values of the brand, functional and emotional needs the brand promises to satisfy, personality of the brand, and distinguishing supporting features of the brand.

In *Guys and Dolls*, the wonderful Frank Loesser musical, Adelaide sings: "You promise me this; You promise me that; You promise me everything under the sun; then you give me a kiss, and you're grabbing your hat, and you're off to the races again."[9]

The promise you make to a specific customer segment is a contract between the customer and brand. It is not something you promise and then "kiss off." It expresses the contract that we make with customers that if they buy our brand, they will receive the promised brand experience. We need to deliver what we promise.

Brand promise is the second P in our Plan to Win. Identifying the promise requires thoughtfulness and creativity. We use a process called the *Brand Pyramid* to help construct the brand promise.

---

[9] Loesser, Frank, "Sue Me," *Guys and Dolls*, 1950.

Brand Pyramid

The Brand Pyramid reflects a simple approach that generates the input used to define the brand promise. It consists of five levels:

- **Brand features**—The bottom level of the Brand Pyramid. The brand features provide the credible support that provides the evidence of the truth of the promise.
- **Functional benefits**—What does this brand do for the target customer?
- **Emotional rewards**—How does this brand make the target customer feel when the functional benefits are delivered?
- **Consumer values**—Who is the target customer in terms of attitudes, beliefs, opinions, interests, and lifestyles?
- **Brand personality**—What is the personality of the brand that differentiates it in the mind of the target customers and makes it so personally appealing?

The functional benefits and the emotional rewards together create the brand claim. The brand values and brand personality together create the brand character.[10] We create the brand promise using the brand claim and the brand character.

We creatively extract the brand promise from the words, thoughts, and ideas in each level of the Brand Pyramid (see Figure 4.2). The brand promise is a statement describing the intended promised experience of your brand. It is a definition of what we want to be. It is our brand aspiration. Combined with input from the segmentation research and other information, only you and your core team as well as select top management can define the vision for the brand. It is not about guesswork. It is about informed judgment.

---

[10] LG Electronics uses a similar approach that is available for review on its corporate Web site. LG discusses how it understands the LG brand in terms of values, promise, benefits, and personality. LG Global Web site, www.lge.com, May 27, 2008.

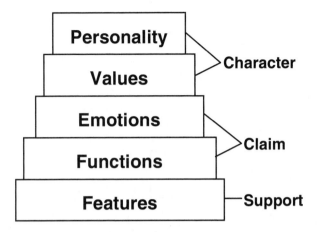

Figure 4.2 Brand Pyramid

We once taught a class using the INSEAD-CEDEP Swatch case.[11] From that document and from newspaper and magazine clippings, we created this Brand Pyramid example for the Swatch brand (see Figure 4.3).

Combined with consumer insight, and input from executives, the next step is to synthesize this information, apply it to understanding your Brand Pyramid, and then complete the following Brand Promise contract (see Table 4.1).

TABLE 4.1 Brand Promise Contract

For people with these values...	
Who seek these rewards...	
Our brand, with this personality...	
Is best at providing these benefits...	
Because it has these features...	

---

[11] INSEAD-CEDEP, 1987, Distributed by ECCH at Babson Ltd., Babson College, Babson Park, MA; Taylor, William, "Message and Muscle: An Interview with Swatch Titan Nicolas Hayek," *Harvard Business Review*, March-April 1993.

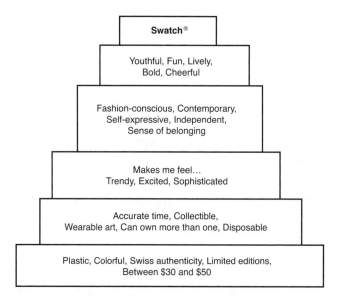

Figure 4.3   Brand Pyramid example for the Swatch brand

Over the years, many of our clients have gone through this process to help restore relevance by updating the promise of a brand that had lost its way.

Nissan

In 1999, we used this process with Nissan as the first brand-focused step in Carlos Ghosn's original three-year plan to turn around the Nissan brand. Mr. Ghosn believed strongly in the use of cross-functional, cross-geographic teams. As bland and fragmented as the Nissan brand was in 1999, the outcome of the Brand Pyramid-Brand Promise initiative created a framework that the design team followed both for the Nissan brand and its sibling brand, Infiniti.

At Nissan, the brand promise guided store design, the design of the corporate headquarters lobby, and the training of employees and sales associates on the showroom floor.

Brand Essence

Defining the brand promise is an important strategic step for revitalizing brand relevance. But, to communicate this idea to the organization, we need to find a shorthand way of stating it, a way that will instantly provide a tonality and attitude to all employees, all communications, and all restaurants and their owners. You might call it a rallying cry; we call it a *brand essence*.

The brand essence captures the core spirit of the brand. It is a compelling and essential phrase. It is the phrase that unambiguously states how we are relevantly differentiated from our competitors. It is a phrase that describes what motivates our customers.

McDonald's Brand Essence

The essence of the McDonald's brand was to appeal to the child in our hearts. McDonald's had to change from a childish brand to a brand that was more aspirational. The new brand essence was focused on appealing to those who are young adults at heart. Those who are younger aspire to be older. And, those who are older don't want to be older.

The simple phrase that expressed this new brand essence of McDonald's was defined as "Forever Young." Brand Essence describes who we are and what we want to be.

Brand Essence Dictionary

It is not enough to define the brand essence. It is also important to define what we mean by that phrase. We call this the *brand essence dictionary*. The dictionary defines the several dimensions of meaning of the brand essence.

Lotus Blossom

A common language with common meanings for commonly used words and phrases is really just good common sense. We should all mean the same things when we say the same things.

We use this Lotus Blossom tool to identify the four to six key words that will help further define the brand essence. It ensures that we create a common book of language so that, regardless of who the employees are, where the employees reside, or what language they speak, we all have a consistent interpretation of the brand.[12]

For example, CNBC's "World Wide Exchange" program, on May 19, 2008, presented an interview with David Procter, CEO, Al Khaliji Bank. He mentioned that his bank was ready for a variety of growth opportunities and that these opportunities meshed with the bank's five core values: Bold, Cool, Swift, Exciting, and Reliable. It was as if the Lotus Blossom with the five dimensions of the bank's brand were filled in (see Figure 4.4).[13]

For one client, we interviewed 86 people at all levels of the organization. We asked each person to define a phrase commonly used in the organization—a phrase that is at the heart of what the brand stands for. There were 86 different ways of defining this critically important phrase. Inconsistent interpretation leads to inconsistent implementation.

The brand essence along with the dimensions in the brand dictionary guide training, product development, marketing, store design, and so forth. With "Forever Young" as the brand goal for McDonald's, we needed to make sure that the interpretation of this simple phrase was consistent around the world.

Brand Essence Discipline

What is the disciplined process for defining the brand essence and its dimensions? There is none. It is a stroke of creativity that comes from intuitively understanding the Brand Pyramid, the brand promise, the market cube, the consumer information, and the vision

---

[12] For a full description of the Lotus Blossom technique, see Higgins, James M., *101 Creative Problem Solving Techniques: The Handbook of New Ideas for Business*, Winter Park, FL: New Management Publishing, 1994, 144.

[13] "World Wide Exchange," CNBC, interview with David Procter, May 19, 2008.

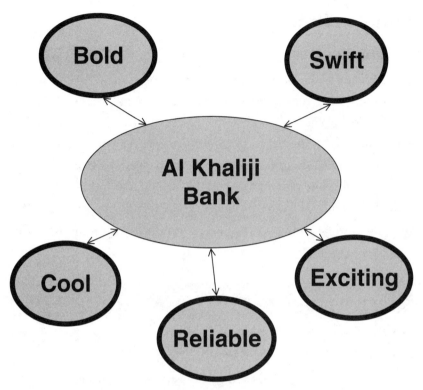

Figure 4.4   Lotus Blossom example for Al Khaliji Bank

for the brand. But, informed insight is not guesswork. There are, however, four guiding principles:

- Base this on a consumer insight.
- Be consistent with Brand Pyramid and brand promise.
- Use as much information as possible.
- Creatively synthesize the information.

At McDonald's, the brand essence was born from reviewing hundreds of documents, including research studies, speeches, articles and books on McDonald's, books on food and eating, a press clipping file from 1990 to 2002, online information searches, and selected interviews with executives at McDonald's, a few who had worked closely with Ray Kroc. It took a synthesist to see what the brand essence was.

Paradox Promise

Often the best expression of a brand essence is a *paradox promise.* The concept of the paradox promise underpins many brands' promised experience. Consumers hate to trade-off benefits. If you want to drink a diet cola, it is certainly much better to have one that has only 1 calorie and also tastes great. Madge the manicurist once promised for Palmolive dishwashing liquid, "It's hard on dishes. It's soft on your hands." Miller Lite defined the light beer market as promising "Great taste. Less filling." Paradox promises can be terrific opportunities. It is worth a lot when you own a paradox promise in the customer's mind.[14]

> ## Paradox Promises
>
> - Fun and functional—Mazda Miata
> - Collectible art and great value—The Franklin Mint
> - Low fat/fewer calories and great taste—Lean Cuisine
> - Refreshing taste and no calories—Diet Coke
> - High-tech, cool, and easy to use—Apple IMac
> - Waterproof and breathable—Gore-Tex
> - Individuality and fitting in—The Gap
> - European luxury, latest technology, and Japanese reliability—Lexus

---

[14] For an interesting perspective on paradox promise, namely Reingold, Jennifer, "Target's Inner Circle," *Fortune*, March 31, 2008: "Target markets itself to the Lexus set as a designer haven while at its core it makes money selling commodities such as bleach and cereal." A former Target executive is quoted as saying, "People have within themselves a paradox. Fit in and belong; and also stand out and be unique. Target does both: mass and class."

McDonald's Paradox Promise

Our insight was that McDonald's represented a paradox promise opportunity.

The striking juxtaposition of opposites led to the insight of the essence of McDonald's being a promised experience that is:

- Familiar yet modern
- Global yet local
- Simple yet enjoyable
- Comfortable yet entertaining
- Consistent yet changing
- Superior quality yet very affordable

With these paradoxes unveiled, the brand essence that focused the new direction for McDonald's was that it represented youthful exuberance yet had strong roots. The brand challenge was to maintain and strengthen McDonald's distinctive heritage and make it relevant again. We saw that one of the things that would make McDonald's so wonderful was that its core values could be relevant forever but their interpretation had to change with the times. The brand challenge was to keep McDonald's "Forever Young" forever.

A relevant brand promise and brand essence can align a disparate organization and provide inspiration and focus. The brand promise is the statement of the promise that the brand will deliver to every customer, every time, everywhere.

The Do's and Don'ts of Restoring Relevance

Do

- **Gain superior understanding of the customer**—Know your target customer better than your competitors. Make sure that you have a clear definition of your target market(s). You should be able to describe your priority segment customers as if they were your best friends.

- **Be inspiring**—Make sure the brand promise statement is compelling and motivating, even or especially in hard times. People want uplift, not undertow.

- **Create three-dimensional market segmentation**—Segmenting on what, who, why, or context each alone is insufficient. Life is not one-dimensional; people are not one-dimensional; and so neither should your segmentation be one-dimensional.

- **Have a consumer-based view of the marketplace**—Let your customers' needs and unmet needs create the competitive set. You will be surprised. Understand your brand's perception by market segment.

- **Synthesize your information**—Go beyond just mere analysis to gain some ideas about the future opportunities and promise of your brand. Generate some critical insights. Be consumer-insight driven.

- **Prioritize your segments**—Apply focus to the mini cubes and make decisions based on your capabilities, future capabilities, value of each segment, and insights into which hold the potential for your brand. You cannot focus on everything at once. As with everything in life, pick your battles wisely.

- **Create your Brand Pyramid and brand promise**—Even if you have one, review it using this format. Keeping a brand contemporary and in sync with the current viewpoints and insights is essential to your brand's health. And remember, this is not filling in the blanks: You are crafting something that will live with your brand for a long time.

- **Conduct competitive analysis within segments**—Understand the competitive sets from your customers' perspective.

- **Use your needs-based segments as windows on the world**—There are opportunities in the identified market cubes. You are really segmenting for innovation and for ideas. Somewhere inside each cube is a terrific new concept.

Don't

- **Don't promise genericization**—Being generic, offering generic category benefits leads to being a commodity product with no relevant differentiation. When you stand for everything general, you stand for nothing special.

- **Don't conduct template management**—Template management is not brand management. Template management lacks passion and understanding. It means you are fabulous at filling in forms. Be passionate about every word and phrase in your Brand Pyramid and brand promise.

- **Don't maintain a mass market mentality**—Especially in today's world, this is death-wish marketing. Mass market messages lead to genericization.

- **Don't be trapped by a nonviable set of segments**—Choose your segments wisely based not only on your insight and foresight but also on your current policies and resource capabilities. And, don't fall on your sword for segments that make no sense.

- **Don't believe that anyone can be a creative synthesist**—Anyone can draw, but how many Monets do you have on your team? Find the synthesist in your ranks or hire one. Do not spend money on creative trainers. Sure, it is a lot of fun to juggle and play games off-site, but true creativity through synthesis is something that only certain people can do.

5 Rule #3: Reinvent the Brand Experience

"The smile on our people's faces is a vital part of our image."
—*Ray Kroc, Grinding It Out*

Brands are promises of relevant and differentiated experiences. The total brand experience (functional and emotional) defines the distinctiveness of the brand.

For example, Lexus redefined luxury in the automotive category. Lexus is more than a well-made, luxurious, technologically advanced vehicle. It also provides a superior purchase and total ownership experience.

Swatch redefined the watch experience. All of sudden a watch was something to be changed with every new outfit, every new mood, any occasion. And it was possible because these colorful, hip, collectible pieces of wrist-candy were affordable.

Ray Kroc knew that for McDonald's to be successful, it had to promise more than burgers, fries, and malts served fast and cheap; it had to be a superior experience. In its early days, it offered a sense of theater, too: It was alive; it was a vibrant, bustling experience. There was the teamwork and camaraderie of the crew, the aroma of the food, the smiles, the exuberance, the uplifting vitality, and the anticipation of excitement as you opened the doors under the Golden Arches. As one of Ray Kroc's early commercials said, "McDonald's is a hap, hap, happy place."

However, as detailed in Chapter 1, "Background to the Turn-around," by 2002, this extraordinary brand experience had deteriorated. Crew people were not proud and happy to be working at McDonald's, and it showed. The crew performed the tasks they were taught without enthusiasm. Camaraderie was replaced by cold routine. An updated version of *Miriam-Webster's Collegiate Dictionary* added a pejorative word, "McJob" meaning "a low-paying dead-end job."

To reinvigorate the McDonald's brand, we would have to re-create, recompose, recontemporize, reinspire, and refocus the entire system on providing a quality product, a clean restaurant, a service mindset, and good value for the money. The organization had to galvanize behind the drivers of operational excellence and leadership marketing. We had to reinvent the brand experience.

Reinventing the brand experience requires several actions within the organization. It is the role of the leaders to instill a set of practices across all functions. These are as follows:

- Commit to an innovation program
- Perform renovation
- Focus on marketing
- Generate customer-perceived fair value
- Bring the total brand experience to life

Each of these practices affects all of the five action Ps in the Plan to Win. As discussed in Chapter 7, "Rule #5: Rebuild Brand Trust," the Plan to Win is the tool for enabling organizational alignment. You must apply all these practices to each of the action Ps detailed in the following list:

- People
- Product
- Place
- Price
- Promotion

So, for example, ask what kinds of product innovations can I make that will enhance the value perception of my brand? What does this change to the lighting outside the restaurant do for the total brand experience?

Brand purpose and brand promise provide the focused direction for the Plan to Win. Now, we have to ask: How do we bring the brand experience to life? How do we deliver the brand promise to achieve the brand purpose? The five action Ps are the key areas that contribute to activating the brand. Actions in all five areas are critical factors for brand revitalization and organizational alignment.

People

Just because a business is customer-focused does not mean that customers come first. Customers come second. Employees come first. That is why "People" is the first action P.

Employees are the frontline when it comes to customer relationships, especially in a service business. Internal brand pride is a critical success factor affecting external brand attitudes. You cannot reinvent the brand experience if your people are not proud and inspired to be a part of the new brand direction. And the leadership must lead. HR has a huge role to play in brand revitalization.

If we want our employees to love our brand, we have to love our employees. If we want our employees to have passion and pride in our delivering a superior brand experience, we have to show them we have passion and pride in what they do and who they are.

Horst Schulze, founding president and former COO of The Ritz-Carlton Hotel Company knew this. An important part of the revitalization of the Ritz-Carlton brand was a redefinition of the brand purpose. He expressed it as "Ladies and gentlemen serving ladies and gentlemen." This became the core concept guiding the behavior of Ritz-Carlton employees.

"The Ritz-Carlton is so intent on empowering their employees to 'wow' customers, each employee (they always refer to their staff members as 'ladies and gentlemen') has permission to spend up to $2,000 a day per guest to fulfill expressed or unexpressed wishes."

"...the company's most successful customer service policies revolve around hiring and empowering their own employees."[1]

If your people do not believe in the brand, then you cannot expect your customers to believe in the brand. This has implications beyond just organizations that do business in a service sector. Brand leadership is top-down. People do not just follow what the leader says, they follow the leader's attitudes and behaviors.

A company gets only one chance to make a first impression, so don't squander the first 72 hours. When a new employee is hired, the first 72 hours are a unique opportunity to instill a positive brand attitude. The "on-boarding" experience sets the stage for the training that follows.

For example, at Disney, every employee is a "cast member." They are all part of the Disney show. Disney takes the hiring process seriously with a series of interviews. They start by hiring people who like people. They make sure prospective employees know what is involved and what is expected of them. Regardless of the role they are to play, all new employees take the one-day *Traditions 1* course. It includes an introduction to company values and customs. It also includes exercises in how to treat "guests" and how to improve their experience. This is followed by training in the park. The emphasis is on human skills.[2]

Disney is clear about its values and priorities. Safety is first, courtesy is next, show or the quality of the product is third, and efficiency is fourth. Customer service doesn't come from a policy manual; it

---

[1] Gray, Audrey, "Welcome to Service," *Dealerscope*, December 2006.
[2] Heskett, et al, *Service Breakthroughs*, Free Press, 1990.

needs to come from an individual's heart. People need to internalize those values and believe in them. As Walt Disney's brother Roy said, "When values are clear, decisions are easy."[3]

Walt Disney, like Ray Kroc, believed in the customer and believed in crafting the best possible experience for that customer. "Walt Disney had a passion for his customer, 'the guest,' to make the experience the very best he possibly could. He believed that if he took care of the front-line experience and service, the bottom line would follow. He embraced a four-tiered philosophy: Dream, Believe, Dare, and Do."[4] Disney spends two weeks training custodial staff, not because sweeping is difficult, but because they are frequently approached by guests with park questions.[5]

The Ritz-Carlton, Disney, and McDonald's are not exceptions just because they are in the service business. Every business needs employees who love the brand.

Just because a restaurant is in the fast food industry, does not mean that employees cannot be proud of the experience. At Chipotle, many crew members will tell you how much they love their jobs. They will explain that working at Chipotle is not merely a job; it is a career. Chipotle offers employees an open door to success.

Chipotle has one of the most inspiring front lines in the fast food category. Proud employees produce a better product and customer experience.

In 2006, Chipotle, recognizing the critical role that the restaurant manager plays, initiated its Restaurateur program to "encourage high-performing general managers to stay with their restaurants rather

---

[3] Broz, Joan, "Management Expert Explains the Disney Way," *Chicago Daily Herald*, D3 edition, March 1, 2007.

[4] Ibid.

[5] Valenzuela, Peter, "How to Keep Good Staff from Leaving; Methods of Human Resource Management in the Health Care Industry," *Physician Executive*, July 1, 2007.

than seek greater earning potential and responsibilities as area managers or with other companies."[6]

"In addition to regular bonuses tied to meeting personal and restaurant-level performance goals, GMs in the program are eligible for a $10,000 bonus for developing hourly workers into managers, and a 10% bonus on revenue gains above a unit's sales projections." This means, for example, that a manager who earns, let's say, "$47,000 a year could potentially earn closer to $100,000 if the branch restaurant has a target of $1.6 million in sales for the year."[7]

Chipotle employees are one of the more significant factors for its success. As one General Manager said, "I'm extremely happy with Chipotle. Every day I wake up, I can't wait to be here, be with my staff. The money will come by itself. If they are happy, if the store is running well, if you are happy and not asking for anything, it will come by itself."[8]

Chipotle Restaurateurs

"A year into the program, Chipotle's first restaurateur topped the $100,000 mark on sales performance alone. Chipotle's management turnover is now below 30%, compared with 34% in 2006, and well below the industry average of 39%. Beyond the money, several restaurateurs say they appreciate the recognition that they can run the restaurant as if it's their own."[9]

At McDonald's, reinventing the people P meant restoring Ray Kroc's service mindset, and this meant restoring pride by reinventing training, support, and rewards. The goal was to not only ensure that employees loved working at McDonald's, but also that they tell others to work for McDonald's as well.

---

[6] Berta, Dina, "Chipotle Incentive Program Aims to Keep, Promote GMs," *Nation's Restaurant News*, November 5, 2007.
[7] Ibid.
[8] Ibid.
[9] Davis, Joyzelle, "Six-Figure Income Possible at Chipotle," *Rocky Mountain News*, August 21, 2007.

We focused on instilling a sense of pride by making sure employees were proud of where they worked; proud of what McDonald's does as an organization; proud of the food offerings; proud to eat the food offerings, simply proud to be a part of McDonald's. Never underestimate the power of employee pride.

McDonald's has more than 1.5 million employees. Turning many of these into brand ambassadors creates a powerful force. Reinventing the people P does not just mean focusing on the crew and the store managers. It meant everyone.[10]

Six Principles of Pride

Charlie Bell used to say that revitalizing marketing leadership at McDonald's meant that our people must be:

- Proud of where we work
- Proud of what we do
- Proud to wear the McDonald's pin
- Proud of our food offerings
- Proud to eat our food offerings
- Proud to be part of McDonald's

Once the executional expression of "Forever Young" was created—"i'm lovin' it"—the goal at McDonald's was to make both the customer and employee experience an "i'm lovin' it" experience. This is a high standard. But why aim for anything less?

Lexus describes its "covenant" with the customer as a goal to "build the finest cars ever built. Lexus will treat each customer as we would a guest in our home." They go on to say that they "will revolutionize the luxury motoring experience through passionate commitment to the

---

[10] There has been a great deal of discussion in the press recently about wearing a "flag pin." Charlie Bell believed that employees should be so proud to work at McDonald's that they would never be embarrassed to wear the McDonald's pin on their lapel, suit jacket, sweater, dress, or shirt.

finest products and the most satisfying automobile ownership experience. We vow to value the customer as an important individual; to do
things right the first time; and to always exceed expectations. We
brought together these principles in the Lexus Covenant, which
inspires our dealers and associates to treat customers as they would
treat guests and to go to any lengths to serve them better."[11]

It was our goal to make the "i'm lovin' it" experience a hallmark of
McDonald's: to restore it as our competitive advantage. To do this, we
understood that we had to earn and re-earn our hospitality reputation
every day, one customer at a time, 47 million times a day.

As mentioned previously, Disney believes that those first
moments happen only once. You only get one chance to make a first
impression. Unfortunately, my first hours at McDonald's were off-
putting and had no connection to the brand.

You Always Remember Your First Time

My first 72 hours at McDonald's were a squandered opportunity.

I still recall my first day at McDonald's. My first meeting included
an introduction to my office location and an introduction to using the
computer network. Over the next three days, I was told how to use
the e-mail system; given a variety of passwords to access my computer, e-mail, intranet, the server, and voice mail; and provided with a
description of the McDonald's medical benefits. This was followed by
an explanation of the executive vehicle plan. Then I had a meeting on
how to use my new mobile phone. I had to learn another password.
That was the extent of my indoctrination. That was it!

I was to be the "brand guy." Yet, I received no presentation on
McDonald's brand heritage. I heard nothing to help me feel proud of
my new employer. There was no help in answering the questions of

---

[11] Lexus Web site, lexus.com; personal experience: as a former Lexus owner, I spent
years as the recipient of their extraordinary customer service.

friends, "So, how do you like it at McDonald's?" I did not receive indoctrination into the McDonald's culture, its values, and its vision. Nothing. I was not given any presentation on the mission or the plans for the future. There was nothing except the implication: Just get to work.

So, as part of brand revitalization, we (global marketing) worked with Rich Floersch (human resources) to reinvent the McDonald's "on-boarding" experience. It was called, "Learnin' it. Livin' it. Lovin' it." The program was designed to make the "welcome-on-board" experience welcoming, informative, inspiring, warm, and fun.

Service Training

Of course, the in-restaurant service aspect is critical. Charlie Bell repeated again and again that we had to be committed to hiring, training, and cultivating people. We need to ensure that people are focused on best service. Employees must not only deliver fast, friendly, accurate service...but also do it with the McDonald's spirit of hospitality.

Consumers cited poor service as a key reason for not returning to McDonald's. Since people deliver the service at McDonald's, there was an urgent need to develop and ingrain the hospitality mindset while still offering the McDonald's high standards of speed. Such things as basic-operations training that had been moved out to the field were reintegrated into the curriculum at Hamburger University. Under Rich Floersch's leadership of the HR function, Hamburger University was reinvigorated. Attendance increased by more than 40%. A commitment to interactive e-learning as a relevant tool for the workforce ensured worldwide training consistency. The concept of quality service is more than just serving people as fast as possible.

The heart of the McDonald's training system is Hamburger University, which is where 5,000 to 7,000 store managers are trained each year. Hamburger University is housed in a 130,000-square-foot building at the corporate headquarters in Oak Brook. Built in 1983, it is in a tranquil setting on 80 acres, complete with two man-made lakes. Inside are four theater-style classrooms, a 300-person auditorium, 20 seminar rooms, three working restaurant labs, and various offices. Translation booths are at the back of classrooms.[12]

A staff of "professors" teach the essential elements of running and managing restaurants. More in-depth business training comes from outside instructors.

Many of the foreign visitors to Oak Brook are there for advanced management training. The basics are often taught through satellite operations using curriculum crafted in Oak Brook and customized as needed for local consumption. McDonald's operates six satellite universities around the world.

The universities have a core curriculum used in hundreds of regional training centers globally.[13]

McDonald's keeps tabs through a series of tracking methods. It begins with basic bookkeeping measures: How many people have taken training, what classes they took, and whether every shift manager is certified in safety.

Tracking then moves up in sophistication as McDonald's seeks to measure the results of its training. Students take competency tests after completing classes. Participants and bosses give feedback on how the training worked. Finally, review teams visit and evaluate restaurants. The process includes "mystery shoppers" who drop in unidentified at stores around the globe.[14]

Service hospitality is about adding something good to each person's day, in small, incremental welcome ways. Restaurant managers were exposed to critical learning programs on hospitality. Test projects on improving the service experience through superior QSC were

---

[12] *Workforce Management* online, www.workforce.com, May 2006.
[13] Galagan, Pat, "Old school gets new role," *T&D Magazine* (2006), 60(11):36.
[14] Ibid and Galagan, Pat and Bingham, Tony, "Training: they're lovin' it," *T&D Magazine* (2006), 60(11):29.

initiated. Other programs for celebrating employees to reduce employee turnover were introduced.

Lifetime of Skills

Unlike years past, most of today's employees are not looking for the promise of a valuable lifetime job. But they do want to gain valuable life experiences. They want valuable experiences that will help them throughout their lives—different jobs, different companies, different organizations, different places. And, they want to be proud of their job, workplace, and company.

Google is one of those companies that encourage employees to learn and grow while continuing to contribute to the corporation. "Google is in tune with the increasing importance today's graduates place on work-life balance. Google culture is geared toward individuals who want to use innovation and creativity to make a tangible difference in the organization. We're looking for people who are really thinking differently and out of the box, who want to do something that has an impact on the world. Every Google employee is encouraged to spend 20% of his or her time developing a new project, a practice that has already resulted in such Google innovations as Google News, Gmail, Google Talk, Orkut, and Froogle."[15]

Nike is another example of a company where you learn as your inherent skills are nurtured. "The company's 'hit the ground running' culture meant that young staffers are granted the opportunity for strong lateral and upward mobility. 'There isn't an incubation period. Nike doesn't wait for you to hit 28 years old in order to recognize you as a valid employee,' says Ben Elkin, university-relations manager at Nike. Although most employees get their start at Nike's Beaverton [Ore.] world headquarters, there are opportunities anywhere—from European sales to running basketball programs in China. Nike

---

[15] "They Love It Here, and Here and Here," *Business Week Online*, B-School News, June 4, 2006.

staffers are engaged in the company's ongoing discussions about corporate social responsibility."[16]

PricewaterhouseCoopers, the accounting firm, has a reputation for imbuing employees with skills. As one new employee stated, "[The company] gives you a good basis for anything that you want to do in life." Ernst & Young is another company with the same understanding of growing personal skills for a lifetime: "In return for my efforts, I like that they're (E&Y) willing to provide me with opportunities to grow personally and professionally within the firm," says Jasmine Rieder, once an intern now an employee full time.[17]

We wanted employees to feel proud again to work at McDonald's, proud that they were acquiring skills that could last them a lifetime, and proud enough to recommend to their friends that they apply for work at McDonald's, too. This can be accomplished, even in the fastfood industry. Chipotle has made a significant commitment to increasing employee pride, and it is working. Naturally, people who look for work want money, benefits, and security. But they also want to feel good about themselves. If we wanted to achieve our brand purpose that McDonald's would be our customers' favorite place and way to eat, we had to make sure that McDonald's would be our employees' favorite place and way to work.

Internal Marketing

Internal marketing is a necessity. External plans and programs will not be as successful if you put the outside world before your own people. Employees come first.

When we launched the global "i'm lovin' it" campaign, we launched it internally first, before a single consumer saw the advertising and experienced the marketing. We demonstrated that our people were the most important elements for making the revitalization of

---

[16] Ibid.

[17] Ibid.

the McDonald's brand work. We wanted "i'm lovin' it" to become an internal rallying cry, not just an external slogan.

Charlie Bell understood this intuitively. As a 15-year-old crew member in Australia, he saw firsthand the importance of great McDonald's service. He understood the difference that exceptional service could make. He recognized that proud employees providing great service can make an indelible impression, and that impression will have impact on a customer's loyalty.

Top Management Matters

For guidance, people look up not down. Leaders must lead. They must inspire. They must recognize and reward producing the right results the right way. When we say the people P, we do not just mean front-line employees.

One company with which we worked ran brand education seminars every year to infuse employees with the new brand policies agreed to by the board of directors. These three-day training sessions were designed to inculcate new brand concepts, new processes, new disciplines, new tools, and new metrics throughout the organization. These sessions were held in nice, off-site locations. The attendees received messenger bags embroidered with the logo for the event including souvenirs and binders of take-home materials. The content was interesting. The food was good. The location was excellent. The evenings were fun-filled. The sessions got excellent reviews. Surveys and follow-ups indicated that the sessions were well received.

After these sessions ended, people traveled back to their respective geographies, and it was business as usual. When they returned to their everyday work nothing changed.

When people looked up to management, they realized that there were the same timetables to meet, the same numbers to achieve. All of this "brand stuff" was just getting in the way of the "realpolitik" of business. The lessons imparted were irrelevant in the grand organizational scheme of things. The leadership did not lead.

Brand revitalization will not work if the employees think that the leadership does not really buy into the concepts and demonstrate that they are true believers. The franchisees and owner/operators would not have been committed if they saw a management in Oak Brook that preached business as usual.

Employees, store managers, owners, suppliers, and everyone in touch with the brand and in touch with the brand's customers take their direction from top management. Top management must demonstrate commitment to the new brand direction if a revitalization of the brand spirit is expected.

McDonald's was committed to revitalizing the brand spirit of the employees. For example, in the restaurant business, the key employee is the restaurant manager. The company recognized the need to restimulate its restaurant managers and rebuild brand pride. I spoke at the first-ever McDonald's global conference for store managers that took place in Sydney in 2004, attended by store managers from 37 countries.

Product

Customers are the lifeblood of any business. Customers are not stupid. They recognize when brands lose their way and go astray. Customers are clear: If they are going to spend hard-earned money for a brand, it had better be a relevant brand promising and delivering superior customer-perceived value. Products and services are the tangible evidence of the truth of the promise.

Jaguar has always been a smaller, niche brand. Over time, due to quality malfunctions and enormous service bills, Jaguar lost all but its core group of devotees. Its customer base shriveled. Ford bought it and tried to revive it but recently threw in the towel, selling it to Tata Motors in India.

The McDonald's customer base was also shrinking. There were many reasons for this but a key reason, as we have previously emphasized, was that the brand lost relevance among its customer base, and new customers saw no real reason to try it. Competition had generated more food buzz, more food news. If we wanted to revitalize the brand, the reinvention of the menu was essential.

Growing customer visits became a business priority. To score dramatic growth, we not only had to increase visits by current customers, we had to gain new customers. We had to convince the unconvinced; we had to attract people who were not currently disposed to visiting McDonald's. Loyalty would ensure that we get a sustainable profitable return on our investment.

We had to give customers and potential customers the opportunity to change their minds about McDonald's. New food news provides this tangible opportunity for people to change their minds.

News Changes Minds

An attitude is an accumulation of information about something resulting in a predisposition to act in a positive or negative way. Attitudes are resistant to change. To change the predisposition, we must change the base of the information on which the predisposition is based.

Apple excites its customers every year with new, coveted products. The TV and cable networks announce new shows every season. Tide is renovated year to year with new varieties (for example, Tide with Bleach) and new products (Tide to Go).

For people to continue to be interested in a brand and for people to think of a brand differently, they must learn something new; for people to change their behavior, they must perceive something new that is relevant. People need permission to change their minds. Learning something new provides the permission for people to change their minds. For McDonald's, the critical news driver had to be "food news."

Renovation and Innovation

Continuous renovation and innovation are imperatives for success. Product and service renovation and innovation are both essential to enduring profitable growth.

With the passionate leadership of Fred Turner and the support of Mike Roberts, McDonald's rededicated its efforts to restoring a passion for product quality. As part of McDonald's previous cost-management focus, product and service quality had been cut. Fred led the way in restoring McDonald's core products to the original "gold standard" of quality. To achieve the new brand purpose to be our customers' favorite, we had to ensure that the food and beverages would be our customers' favorites. Some of the food improvement initiatives were as follows:

- Improving the taste of the burger through new seasoning and improved cooking and holding procedures
- Better buns and a return to proper toasting of the buns
- New equipment and procedures to serve better quality food
- Improving the quality of the coffee

In addition to the products for which McDonald's was famous, consumers wanted more choices. This is not unique to McDonald's. In today's environment, the proliferation of choice is a marketing fact of life. Look at the snack chip/pretzel aisle; just try to buy a toothbrush; observe the enormous amount of options in the beverage aisle. In this choice-demanding world, McDonald's menu was too limited in appeal.

Product News at McDonald's

Iconic new products are an important contributor to brand revitalization. These icons are tangible evidence of the brand's commitment to change. For Nissan, the icon that launched the brand revival was the relaunch of the "Z" in 2002. For Apple, it was the relaunch of the iMac computer and later the launch of the iPod. For GE, it is the investment in innovative technology demonstrating corporate commitment to environmental responsibility; for Toyota, the launch of the Prius demonstrated leadership and true commitment to delivering greater fuel efficiency.

In response to criticism that McDonald's did not have any nutritious options on its menu, the iconic new product introduction of salads in early 2003 helped to launch the message that McDonald's is relevant again: a line of salads endorsed by Paul Newman served with "Newman's Own" all-natural salad dressing. A great-tasting salad on the McDonald's menu helped to provoke people to think that McDonald's is really changing.

The salad introduction was focused on young adult moms. While it is clear that a lot of people were eating salads, not just young adult moms, this focus gave the offer a specific appeal to a specific audience that gave the new product credibility.

When moms brought their kids to McDonald's, a large percentage did not order food for themselves. So, salads were marketed to appeal to young adult moms as a natural way to get an immediate sales response. After all, she was already in the restaurant. With the availability of salads, yogurt, apple slices, and water, there was an opportunity for parents to not only buy food for themselves but also to eliminate the parental "veto power" when it comes to the decision of where the kids will eat.

McDonald's success with new products had not been very good. History was littered with notable product failures such as McLean or Salad Shakers. In 1998, *BusinessWeek* reported that McDonald's last successful new product was the Chicken McNugget launched in 1983: "In the '90s, the company has careened from tests with pizza and veggie burgers to confusing discount promotions such as last year's Campaign 55." Additionally, the article stated, "The company has been unable to harness the strength of its brand to grow beyond its basic formula of burgers and fries."[18]

[18] Leonhardt, David, "McDonald's: Can it regain its golden touch?" *BusinessWeek*, March 9, 1998.

A new approach to new product development was required. Mike Roberts led the way in insisting that a new, disciplined process be adopted. New products are terrific ways to change people's attitudes. But, if operations become bogged down with too many changes, customers will become frustrated and have poor experiences regardless of how fabulous the new food idea.

The results of the new product discipline were remarkable. Not every new idea was successful. For example, the launch of chicken fingers did not meet expectations. However, the odds of success improved significantly. New products such as McGriddles, new salads, improved coffee, chicken snack wraps, and yogurt parfait are significant contributors to McDonald's continued brand revitalization.

New Approach to New Product Development

The previous approach to new product development at McDonald's was to look at the competition and react. The R&D focus was to look for ways to take what we knew how to do and try to convince people that they needed what we knew how to produce.

This approach is not unusual. Many manufacturing companies are loathe to make changes to the existing assembly lines because they cannot have up-front assurance that the new product will be a success. Some appliance manufacturers were in this rut, changing only those superficial components added on post-manufacture such as handles, knobs, and colors.

But, effective marketing is about figuring out what consumers want and then figuring out how to profitably satisfy these wants at better value than competitive alternatives. Instead of beginning with the product, begin with the customer need.

Home Depot reinvented the fire extinguisher. Technically, there's nothing wrong with standard fire extinguishers. But they happen to be eyesores, and eyesores end up hidden, shoved in a closet or otherwise out of reach when a grease fire ignites. The new HomeHero Kitchen

Fire Extinguisher ($30) from Home Depot could help save your house, but not because of any chemical breakthrough. The powder it sprays is similar to baking soda. It simply looks good enough to stay on a counter, in full view, ready to smother a fire before it becomes a blaze.[19] In the process of making the 16-inch-tall HomeHero look more appealing, Home Depot improved on the ergonomics of fire extinguishers. After pulling the safety pin, you can aim and shoot with one hand, pressing the trigger with your thumb. The simple instructions also indicate the two types of fires the HomeHero is designed to put out: grease and electrical.

Dyson reinvented the vacuum cleaner. As we explained in our earlier discussion about segmentation, consumers were frustrated trying to find the right bag for their particular vacuum. Dyson invented the bagless vacuum cleaner. It was so successful that the entire category had to respond with bagless offers.

Putting customer needs first turns the entire approach to innovation on its head. Needs-based market segmentation becomes a key driver for effective product development.

The menu management team, under the leadership of Claire Brabowski, welcomed the concept of needs-based segmentation. Claire became a big internal supporter of this new approach to innovation. Claire not only welcomed the needs-based segmentation, she volunteered to help sell the segmentation into the organization.

Happy Meals

Childhood obesity is a wedge issue in food marketing, and the point of the wedge was aimed at McDonald's. There was a clear need for healthier alternatives as part of the Happy Meal offer.

---

[19] Sofge, Erik, "Quick HomeHero Fire Extinguisher Is One You Don't Have to Hide," *Popular Mechanics*, November 2007.

Jim Cantalupo declared that we needed to demonstrate leadership and not merely react. As a first step, recognizing that parents were looking for more beverage choices with Happy Meals, McDonald's announced that Happy Meals would include wholesome beverage alternatives such as milk, mineral water, Sunny Delight, orange juice, and other fruit juices. In France, there was a yogurt beverage choice (Actimel). In many countries, bottled water was available. In addition some parents said they wanted an alternative to fries. So, McDonald's started offering Apple Dippers, fresh apple slices and seedless grapes in some countries. To become the customer's favorite place and way to eat and drink, the primary focus had to be on food and beverage choices. Chicken McNuggets were improved to be made with whole, white meat chicken.

Place

Place means more than a store. Depending on the business, it can be a Web site, restaurant, office, waiting room, hotel room, customer's office, showroom, shelf space, vans, and trucks. For one of our clients, the "place" is actually your place, your home. That is where the sale is made. Wherever it is, remember place is the face of your brand.

No one likes sitting in an older, dirty airplane. It makes you feel uneasy, uncomfortable, and unsafe. No one likes a smelly, decrepit airline terminal or hotel lobby. Hotel rooms with frayed carpeting and curtains, stained and chipped bathroom tiles, and rust rings in the shower make you feel dirty. Who wants to buy toys from a store where the boxes in the window have turned yellow from years of exposure? And, no one wants to frequent a rundown, out-of-date, restaurant. It affects the eating experience. Customers tend to believe that if you do not care enough about the front of the store, how must you feel, they wonder, about the back of the store—where the food is prepared? Place must attract not detract from your brand.

Nothing happens until it happens at retail. Retail is the moment of truth. It is the most powerful, most intimate, and most credible brand message.

Your place is a brand showplace. Trader Joe's Markets are an example of making the store the brand. The ambiance is relaxed, easy to understand, and friendly. The employees wear their Hawaiian shirts and exude their best beachcomber attitude. The products are designed and labeled creatively. You buy inexpensive products yet you feel as if you are buying something special. The Trader Joe's environment is more laid-back, more intimate, and less intense than a trip to Whole Foods.

The Mumm Napa Vineyards has created a beautiful and elegant brand experience in St. Helena, California. Of course, the vineyards are extraordinary to look at, and yes, there is a tour. But the tasting room is the way they have brought this brand to life: They have created a one-of-a-kind experience that melds the sophistication of the French Mumm experience and the American West Napa-Sonoma experience. You sit at small tables—inside or on an outside deck—overlooking a valley of vines; you are presented with a series of different flights of sparkling wines including some that are new or not available for purchase in most restaurants. You have your own server who is dressed elegantly and explains each of the wines to you as if you are a special guest. On Sunday, there is a brunch. Even though many of their bottles sell for under $20, when you leave, you believe that Mumm Napa *methode champenoise* wines are truly the incarnation of Champagne in America.

Apple stores are brilliant representations of the brand. Reflecting the same design attitude of Apple's iconic products, the store and its employees reflect a basic tenet of Apple that is easy-to-use computing. The excitement of Apple is always on display as the stores are crowded with people eager to belong to Apple and genuinely interested in learning as much as they can about the products and using them.

Starbucks was designed to create a multisensory environment that melded coffee, coffee aromas, and conviviality. In an *Ad Age* piece, Jane Stevenson wrote, "Visitors came to expect a multisensory experience that was replicated in each store, from the sights, sounds, and smells of coffee being ground to the familiar layout, furniture, music, and wireless access. Starbucks merchandized the feeling and the environment."[20]

One of the challenges that Carlos Ghosn set was fixing the Nissan and Infiniti showrooms: Nissan's dealerships, including the signage, had to be updated to reflect the new brand character of Nissan. As Infiniti was the luxury brand, it had to create a luxury showroom experience.

When a customer walks into a McDonald's restaurant, she walks into the brand. The look and feel of the restaurants must represent the new look and feel of the brand. As Paula Moore reported in the *Denver Business Journal*, "McDonald's took a cue from other retailers, such as Starbucks Coffee Co. and Wal-mart Stores, Inc. and now focuses on being a lifestyle purveyor, not just a seller of products."[21]

A multisegment, multidimensional brand like McDonald's requires a multifaceted, multiretail experience. So, to achieve the goal of making the brand the customer's favorite place, the outdated standardized appearance of McDonald's restaurants had to be multifaceted. Led by Denis Hennequin, in France, a new localized, customized approach to store-design was adopted. "'Re-imaging is essential in the competitive world of retail,' said Mr. Hennequin. 'We need to avoid aging faster than our customers.'"[22]

---

[20] Stevenson, Jane, "Use merchandising to build and attract consumers; powerful tool: what and how you sell at the retail level can drive just as much growth as other strategies," *Ad Age*, CMO Strategy column, February 25, 2008, p. 17.

[21] Moore, Paula, "Marble, jazz: is this really McDonald's?" *Denver Business Journal*, August 28, 2006.

[22] Werdigier, Julia, "McDonald's European tour: sales rise as the chain revamps its restaurants on the Continent," *The International Herald Tribune*, August 18, 2007, p. 11.

We had to make the new brand promise come alive in the restaurant. We had to create an internal ambiance that would reflect the vibrant relevance of the new brand promise. The restaurants had to be modernized, not merely dehomogenized. How the restaurants looked not only affected customers but employees as well. People felt proud to work in a reimaged restaurant.

Part of the place changes were the reimaging of the restaurants. But there were other place changes as well.

Reimaging

If the place is the face of the brand, McDonald's needed some face lifts. The redesign of the stores had to stay true to the "Forever Young" spirit of the new brand strategy. This required more than a "sprucing up," more than a "nip and tuck." While keeping the brand values alive forever, McDonald's needed to embrace a contemporary new design for its restaurants to keep the public face of these values "Forever Young." This would be the first time in three decades that McDonald's would undertake such a huge redesign of its restaurants worldwide.

An article in *BusinessWeek* stated: "After 30 years without a major design overhaul, the 51-year-old fast-food giant is adopting a hip new look. The world's largest hamburger chain is redesigning its 30,000 eateries around the globe in a 21st century makeover of unprecedented scale."[23]

BusinessWeek also pointed out that this redesign had to be done. "McDonald's, whose restaurants are visited by more than 40 million people every day, has moved aggressively over the past three years to revamp its menu and attract a new breed of customer. It has added healthier items like premium salads targeted at women, and apple

---

[23] Gogoi, Pallavi, "Mickey D's McMakeover," *BusinessWeek*, May 15, 2006.

slices and skim milk for children. But as more upscale items like Asian chicken salad show up on its menu, the chain's typical starkly lit, plastic-heavy look is at odds with the contemporary, welcoming image the company wants to present. 'McDonald's promises to be a *forever young* brand,' says John Miologos, vice-president of worldwide architecture, design, and construction at McDonald's Corp. 'We have to deliver on that promise.'"[24] The last major change at McDonald's restaurants was the introduction of play places for children in the early 1980s.

"The big red roof looks too dated today," says John Bricker, creative director at design firm Gensler's brand-strategy arm, Studio 585. It's being replaced by a flat roof topped by a newly designed, contemporary, golden sloping curve.[25]

Continuing the story, *BusinessWeek* reported that after conducting a global contest among design firms, the burger giant chose New York-based Lippincott Mercer in the summer of 2004. Peter Dixon, the design firm's creative director, spent 2005 with McDonald's internal architecture and design team testing and prototyping the new look, which is being officially rolled out this year. Lippincott Mercer, which until it signed McDonald's had few clients in the restaurant business, has made a name for itself working with companies going through a shift in brand identity and image. In 2002, for example, it helped redesign Nissan Motor Co. dealerships to reflect the company's launch of several new upscale cars. Within a year, the redesigned dealerships saw an average of 57% sales growth, versus 33% overall.[26]

It is not easy to update more than 30,000 restaurants. But, keeping the face of the brand "Forever Young" is important. Restaurants are billboards—this can be a highly effective advertising.

---

[24] Ibid.
[25] Ibid.
[26] Ibid.

The experience from McDonald's France indicated that modernizing the décor had a positive impact on the entire experience for the customer and boosted sales and profits. Rather than having one dominant design, McDonald's adopted and adapted multiple design concepts to fit the needs of various neighborhoods. Brand standardization was out. Brand customization was in. The belief that every McDonald's can look different, as long as each feels like McDonald's and as long as the experience is a McDonald's experience was a major change in the store design policy.

Cleanliness

Cleanliness was part of Ray Kroc's original mantra: Cleanliness is the "C" in QSC. In the intervening years, as the brand spiraled downwards, the focus on cleanliness became less clear. Charlie Bell was passionate that McDonald's had to become again "the king of clean." He insisted that McDonald's recalibrate cleanliness standards making sure that restaurants would be spotlessly clean with franchised as well as the company-owned restaurants.

McCafé

Charlie Bell's idea of McCafé was another way to reenergize and enhance the McDonald's experience. First executed in Australia/New Zealand, McCafé was generating a lot of buzz and was becoming a successful alternative to other coffee houses and cafés including Starbucks. The McCafé concept was an experiential corner in the restaurant for those who have the need for a more comfortable environment of a premium coffee house. The idea spread to several other countries.

Charlie had a McCafé designed for the lobby of the Oak Brook headquarters to help communicate that there is new thinking at McDonald's. The purpose was to change this first impression from the look and feel of a boring bus station to a new "Forever Young" brand experience. As people entered the lobby, they were instantly confronted with a new brand experience that communicated that McDonald's is innovating again. The headquarters McCafé drew the attention of employees during morning arrival, and allowed employees and visitors to sit and chat at lunch or during an afternoon break. It generated an ambiance of "i'm lovin' it" internally within the lobby of McDonald's. It wasn't about sales. It was about delivering a brand message.

The newly designed model McDonald's restaurant near the U.S. headquarters was designed to reflect the new brand experience to the public. It represented the new "Forever Young" brand attitude and also contained a defined coffee area.

Consistent with the original idea of becoming the "favorite place and way to eat and drink," Don Thomson, President of McDonald's USA, remarked at an analyst meeting, "We want to move from beverages as an accompaniment to being a beverage destination." Charlie's vision of the coffee opportunity persisted. Today coffee is a contributor to McDonald's continued sales growth. Charlie also understood that to create the right coffee experience the normal McDonald's front counter was not optimal. While separate McCafé's were adopted in some countries and adapted in others, McDonald's in the United States is refitting the front counter in some restaurants to provide a separate coffee station and to provide both better quality product and service.[27] This is a good example of how a global idea benefits from local customization.

McDonald's restaurants had to be customized differently to meet the needs of these segments in different neighborhoods with different attitudes. Some restaurants had patio eating facilities. Some restaurants had kiosks for downloading movies and music.

---

[27] "Coffee clash: McDonald's takes on Starbucks," November 18, 2007, www.msnbc.msn.com.

Drive-Thru

Then there is the drive-thru. The importance of the drive-thru is growing. In the United States, more than 60% of McDonald's sales are through the drive-thru window.[28] Because of the traffic flow and potential for traffic slow-downs, McDonald's developed and began to implement the idea of double-lane drive-thrus. Even in China, McDonald's launched the drive-thru concept.

The drive-thru brand experience has to be a "Forever Young" experience. Customers are not in the restaurant, so they are not seeing and feeling the new designs or the cleanliness. The challenge for drive-thru is how to establish the experience in such a way that the customer takes that experience with him wherever he is going with the food. This continues to be a challenge.

Community Tables and Other Innovative Designs

Following an idea that began in Europe, some restaurants created "community" tables that appeal to young adults. Others created conversation nooks.

Today, store design is taking on all kinds of new dimensions, most particularly in the area of multisensory marketing using the sense of smell, the sense of hearing with sounds, and so forth. Westin Hotels is using proprietary scent to enhance its brand experience.

Starbucks uses music, as does the retail chain Urban Outfitters. Designing the brand into the place is a serious factor to brand experience revitalization.

In addition to the appearance of the new store designs, McDonald's focused on redesigning the whole experience. This includes the

---

[28] A recent article in *Advertising Age*, reported that "less than a third of fast-food patrons dine in (the restaurant). Repeat business and brand loyalty are thus highly dependent on positive drive-through experiences." Lemonnier, Jonathan, "Your Fast-Food Fix Costs $500 A Year," May 26, 2008.

sounds of the equipment, the appearance of the front counter, a more open look, more contemporary music, plasma screens, and more comfortable seating.

Price

Henry Ford was committed to the mission of creating an affordable automobile. He democratized automotive transportation. Sam Walton built a retail empire making shopping for everyday needs available and affordable. William Levitt of Levittown fame democratized housing by making it affordable to the average home owner. Amadeo Giannini builder of Bank of America democratized banking. Most bank customers today take for granted the things Giannini pioneered, including home mortgages, auto loans, and other installment credit.

A pioneer of the discount brokerage concept, Charles Schwab created one of the most recognized financial names among the general public. Schwab led the revolution to discount brokerage services. Schwab cut its rates while many other brokers raised them.

Ray Kroc's great contribution to the world was to make eating out so affordable that more people could eat out more often. He democratized eating out.

Superior availability and affordability were key contributors to the success of brands like Ford, Wal-Mart, Bank of America, Schwab, and McDonald's. Remember the original McDonald's sign? It announced a "15¢ Hamburger." Ray Kroc knew that McDonald's would not always be able to sell hamburgers for 15¢. But he was committed to the idea that the price should be in direct proportion to what 15¢ was when he started.

Price would always play a role at McDonald's. Price would always be a key strategic lever for the brand. But, how we talk about price is important.

Value is more than just low price. Value is what you get for the price you pay. Marketing leadership means knowing the difference between pricing that demotes the brand and creating value that promotes the brand.

Price and Value

Price is an important part of the customer's value equation. But although part of the value equation, price is not the whole equation.

Defining the functional and emotional brand experience that differentiates the brand is the critical factor determining whether we will be a commodity or a valued brand. Value is the numerator in the brand equation of promised experience for the customer's money and time.[29]

$$\text{Value} = \frac{\text{Functional and Emotional Experience}}{\text{Money and Time}}$$

Toyota understands this. Superior value perception does not just apply to the Corolla. When Toyota introduced Lexus it was not only a luxury experience, it was an affordable luxury experience—not cheap but much less than Mercedes. Lexus promised the best luxury automotive ownership experience for both your money and your time. What Lexus referred to as "the relentless pursuit of perfection," meant more than merely focusing on price. They focused on the whole value equation.

McDonald's had to provide more than just low price and speed to have a competitive advantage. We had to provide a relevant, differentiated experience at prices and convenience that allowed more customers to visit McDonald's more often. It had to be a convenient and fast. But for these visits to generate customer perceived value, we also

---

[29] We have discussed the value equation previously, but it is essential to understand the role price has in brand promise.

had to enhance the experience that can only be generated by operational excellence and leadership marketing.

Fair Value

Value is not just a menu invoice: It is a marketing imperative. Of course, we had to reassure our customers that we were still, as always, affordable. But making a brand affordable does not mean that we should cheapen the brand perception. McDonald's value is not just about the "value menu." The whole menu is a value menu. And, the whole experience determines brand value.

Charlie Bell liked to recall the story of a kid counting coins in the palm of his hand to buy his favorite McDonald's meal. Charlie described this young boy standing in front of the menu board, sorting and stacking his coins in the palm of his hand until he knew he had the right amount. When that boy finally realized that he had enough money clenched in his small fist to purchase and enjoy the food, the kid smiled and knew he was about to have a great McDonald's experience. It was by far the best, most valued purchase that kid made.

Fair Value Corridor

To generate brand value, we build the power of a brand, not exploit the brand power we have inherited. To increase shareholder value, we must be the most efficient and productive provider of a branded offer that customers value.

To build brand value, we must manage the relationship between what customers are willing to pay and the benefits they receive, as we discussed in describing the brand value equation. What is the "fair value" for our offer? Fair value is not determined by the marketer. It is determined by customers.

In Figure 5.1, brands A, B, and C are all perceived to be fair value for the benefits offered. The diagonal in the figure is the *fair-value corridor*. Brands located above the corridor are perceived to be poor value for the promised benefits. And brands located below the corridor are perceived to be superior value.

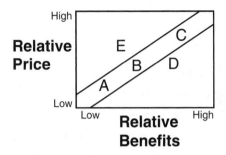

Figure 5.1   Customer-perception fair value map

Target Stores

Target stores in the United States have low prices. But Target also delivers a contemporary brand experience of trendy style. Their brand promise of "chic and stylish that is affordable" differentiates Target in a relevant way from Wal-Mart.[30] As the *Financial Times* reported in May 2005, "Target appears to be running a better business.... Wal-Mart's shares are becoming as cheap as its products."[31]

Don't Build Deal Loyalty

An immediate action for McDonald's was to decrease significantly the excessive marketing communications emphasis on price. Building deal loyalty does not build brand loyalty. Deal loyalty is not real loyalty. Brand loyalty cannot be bought with bribes. All you do is make the customer loyal to the deal instead of loyal to the brand. If there is a better deal elsewhere, deal loyal customers are out your door and in through the competitor's door. If a customer does not

---

[30] Birchall, Jonathan, "What Wal-Mart Women Really, Really Want," *The Financial Times*, October 10, 2005.

[31] "The Lex Column," *The Financial Times*, May 13, 2005.

prefer our brand experience, then making it cheaper and easier will not build our brand. Matt Paull, the CFO, continually emphasized that this type of behavior was the rocky, downhill road to "brand commoditization."

Value Is the Real Deal

Occasionally reminding people that a brand is affordable is important. But excessive emphasis on price alone destroys real loyalty and builds deal loyalty. Instead of the dominant message being about price, to revitalize a brand, the new communications emphasis needs to be on brand relevance.

Promotion

Everything communicates. Promotion is more than tactical programs. Brand promotion is about creating an integrated approach to advocating on behalf of the brand.

Brand Promotion Versus Brand Demotion

Unfortunately, promotion has taken on a limited meaning in marketing. Promotion is often interpreted to mean short-term tactics designed to generate immediate traffic. It is more than "20% off this weekend." It is more than "two for the price of one." It is more than a short-term tactical incentive to buy now.

I am often asked, "How much should we spend on promotion and how much on brand-building?" This is a false dilemma.

We need to go back to the original definition of promotion. To "promote" means to elevate to a higher level, to advance in rank or position. The purpose of all brand communications should be to elevate a brand to a higher level, to advance the brand to a higher position in the customer's mind. According to *Merriam-Webster's Dictionary*, promotion means "the act of furthering the growth or development of something." So, when people discuss the balance of advertising versus promotion, this is a false choice. All marketing communications should promote the brand in a manner that furthers the growth of the brand.

The promotion P in the Plan to Win does not mean a monthly promotional calendar of separate, short-term, disconnected, activities. The promotion P includes every communication about the brand whether it is a game, a tie-in, an advertisement, or a corporate brochure. All brand communications activities need to be executed around a coherent message with a consistent voice promoting the brand to a higher level, furthering the profitable growth of the brand.

The opposite of "promote" is "demote." Unfortunately, a lot of promotions today are not brand promotions. They are brand demotions in disguise, activities that drive the brand's sales at the expense of the brand reputation, all to the detriment of the long-term health of the brand. Excessive reliance on inconsistent, short-term brand messages demotes a brand. Brand demotion does not promote the brand to a higher level; instead it cheapens, confuses, and detracts from brand building.

We cannot demote our brand today and expect a strong brand tomorrow. Disconnected promotional communications lead to incremental brand degradation. Instead of communicating "great price," we need to communicate "great brand at a great price."

An integral and immediate part of the turnaround was to ensure that we created marketing communications programs that promoted the brand to higher levels of customer appreciation. Our campaign strategy for McDonald's was to move from an excessive emphasis on the deal of the month, to a consistent, coherent, integrated brand building message.

Brand Journalism

For mega-brands like McDonald's, Coca-Cola, Kellogg's, GE, Samsung, Sony, HP, and Visa, we need to reinvent the concept of brand positioning by instituting the new concept of *brand journalism*.

Mega-brands are multidimensional, multisegment, multifaceted brands. No one communication alone can tell the whole, multifaceted megabrand story.

USP: Unique Selling Proposition

The concept of *unique selling proposition*, or *USP*, later known as *brand positioning*, is fine for launching new brands and for creating niche brands. But, this old-fashioned view of brand positioning can create a mental lock-box within which there is no leeway for a mega-brand to respond to a changing world.

Think about journalism for a moment. Journalism is the collection and communication of news, events, and happenings. Journalism provides order to otherwise disparate or unconnected events. Journalism informs, entertains, and persuades.

Think of magazines like the newsweeklies. Whether *Time, Newsweek, The Economist, The New Yorker*, or *US News and World Report*, the principle is the same—just as it is with the monthlies such as the *Atlantic Monthly, Vanity Fair*, or *Rolling Stone*. An overarching brand direction defines the common brand character that differentiates each magazine and provides a coherent, integrated vision for the brand. However, each magazine covers a variety of topics that interest a variety of people. The editors do not expect every reader to read every article. Different people with different interests will read different articles. And, at different times in their lives, as people's interests change, they will be interested in reading different articles. Only a few people will be interested in every article in every edition.

It is the same with brand journalism. Brand journalism is a chronicle of the varied things that happen in the brand's world, throughout the day, throughout the years. This is how we create real customer-perceived lifetime value for a brand.

Think about a college student who has declared a major. This student's major is his or her mindset. To satisfy the needs defined by this mindset, the student will take a variety of courses, not all the same but associated with the major. A student can have some liberties within this mindset to add classes that may be off-beat or only tangentially related to the major. And yet, everything is still connected to the overarching essence of that student's mindset.

Now think about McDonald's communications. For McDonald's, this all added up to a distinctive journalistic brand chronicle. We defined a common brand purpose and brand character for the McDonald's brand. We defined a common brand promise. But, the relevance of the promise means different things to different people at different occasions. The motivation to go to McDonald's is different for kids, teens, young adults, parents, and seniors. The appeal of McDonald's is different at breakfast, lunch, dinner, snack time, weekday, and on the weekend, as well as with kids, without kids, or on a business trip. The competitive set is different for different people with different needs in different situations.

A brand journalism approach does not mean changing the overarching brand vision or the brand promise. It does mean appealing to different people with different desires in different contexts. The communications plan consists of a compilation of varied messages, different subjects, and different topics, that all come together in a dynamic, ever-evolving, overall relevant brand story. Brand journalism allows us to express the multidimensional essence of a brand in a way that is appealing and compelling to specific audiences with their specific needs.

Brand journalism requires multimedia communications such as sports, outdoor, indoor, special events, global, local, educational, musical, radio, television, print, online, offline, in the streets, and so forth. This is a challenge. All the various brand messages in various media need to be integrated into a coherent brand story always respecting and imbued with the brand promise.

Media Frenzy

After I first explained the concept of brand journalism, at a June 2004 Advertising Age conference, as not only the new marketing approach for McDonald's, but also as the future world of marketing, the traditionalists struck back creating a mild media frenzy. The staunch traditionalists anchored in the past stood their ground, furiously defending their passé views on positioning. These prophets of the past protested that this new approach to marketing would fail.[32]

The good news for marketing is that there were also those who saw the future coming and who recognized—again in letters to *Advertising Age*—that social trends were pointing to continued fragmentation of culture. Brand journalism was a way to address this "mincemeat society."[33]

At the Association of National Advertisers (ANA) conference in Naples, Florida, later that year, James R. Stengel, global marketing officer of P&G said, "The traditional marketing model we all grew up with is obsolete. We are taking the reinvention of marketing very seriously at P&G and we all need to do that."[34]

Jim Stengel recognized that the narrow focus of Crest as a fluoride toothpaste preventing childhood cavities was limiting the profitable growth potential of the brand. Crest has evolved its brand from a narrow focus on a fluoride toothpaste that prevents cavities among children—"Look, Mom, no cavities." Today, Crest has a mega-brand vision with greater growth potential. The new vision is a lifetime of oral care promising a healthy beautiful smile and fresh breath—"Healthy,

---

[32] Trout, Jack, "Brand Chronicles, Baloney!" Viewpoint, *Advertising Age*, July 19, 2004, p. 18. They were wrong.

[33] Popcorn, Faith, "Light gets it right; cultural change requires a multidimensional approach to marketing," Viewpoint, *Advertising Age*, August 2, 2004, p. 11.

[34] Stengel, James R., as quoted in *The New York Times*, Advertising Column: Stuart Elliott, October 19, 2004.

beautiful smiles for life." This new approach does not just focus on kids. To communicate the new Crest message, different messages in different media designed to interest different people with different needs are required. This brand journalism approach to Crest has helped to revitalize the brand.

As the world changes, outmoded ideas need to be rejected. Hanging on to the traditional marketing model is not the way to create a brand's future.

The "positionistas," as I like to call them, are glued to the glory of an immutable, narrow, unidimensional view of a brand. They believe that brands are simple, single-word ideas. And once this idea is established, they believe that you cannot change people's minds. This is wrong. Brands are complex, multidimensional ideas, and you can change people's minds. McDonald's is a good example. These same people tell us that line extensions are bad. But as the revitalization of Crest demonstrates, these views are wrong.

Line Extensions

Regarding line extensions, the positionistas say that brand extensions threaten brands. This is not always true. A disciplined line extension strategy can strengthen brands. In fact, for mega-brands, line extensions are an important part of the brand growth plan.

Consistent with the redefinition of the Crest brand promise described above, line extensions are now an important part of the Crest brand story. By extending the Crest brand to include a wide variety of dental hygiene products providing cavity protection, tartar protection, sensitive teeth protection, enamel protection, and protection against stains, the brand is stronger, not weaker. There are gels, pastes, teeth whitening pastes, rinses, toothbrushes, strips, and so on. These line extensions strengthen the appeal of the Crest brand. They allow the brand to appeal to different people at different times in their lives.

The brand journalism approach to a "healthy, beautiful smile for life" appeals to more people with a variety of needs throughout the various stages of life. It creates a lifetime brand relationship. It recognizes the profitable growth opportunity of the lifetime value of a customer.

Tide is another P&G brand that evolved from a single-minded powdered detergent brand that promised heavy-duty cleaning to a mega-brand that promises "Tide knows fabrics best." There are liquid versions; cold water versions; versions with bleach, stain removers, fabric softener, and fabric refresher; versions with new scents; and even a portable version that helps to remove food stains on the spot (Tide to Go). These line extensions help to strengthen the brand journalism story of Tide.

What do we learn from all this? Traditional approaches to marketing need to be regularly reassessed. Innovation and renovation apply to marketing.

While market segmentation is a foundational concept of modern marketing, the idea that a brand can be reduced to a single word appealing to only one market segment with only one benefit is wrong for today's marketing world.

Cultural Marketing

Cultural marketing means aiming to make a brand relevant in various cultures. The goal is to embrace individual cultural segments and cross-cultural fusions that are becoming more and more apparent in global society. How do you make an American brand like McDonald's relevant in different cultures such as France, Australia, and China? How do you make a brand like McDonald's relevant to different cultures within the United States? It is important to make a global brand relevant in a wide variety of cultures. Marketing standardization leads to marketing homogenization. Multicultural and multilocal is what we aimed to achieve in the execution of "i'm lovin' it."

"i'm lovin' it"

The phrase and the spirit of "i'm lovin' it" became a universal cultural expression. In the United States, Russia, Denmark, United Kingdom, and China, we witnessed examples of "i'm lovin' it" in popular culture. In Russia, more than 20,000 students participated in a parade featuring "i'm lovin' it" flags, banners, and signs. In Korea, "i'm lovin' it" joggers were seen running through the streets. In China, it became a hand signal.

Consistency Is Critical

The new campaign direction and the executional approach resonated with employees and customers around the world. Mary Dillon became CMO of McDonald's toward the end of 2005. She quickly concluded that the campaign she inherited was still working. There was no reason to change. In 2008, she said, "'i'm lovin' it' is a campaign that has a lot of life ahead of it. Awareness of the words and the five musical notes is about as high as it gets and the likability of it is quite high."[35] This consistency of a campaign idea is in great contrast to previous McDonald's advertising practice. From 1960 to 2002, McDonald's implemented 21 different advertising themes.[36] Lack of consistency creates brand uncertainty. In 2003, McDonald's launched its first-ever global advertising campaign. It is still strong in 2008.

In 2008, Neil Golden became the new CMO for McDonald's in the United States. In an *Ad Age* interview, Neil endorsed the authentic feel of the advertising. He appreciates that the "I" in "i'm lovin' it" represents the voice of the consumer. The "it" in "i'm lovin' it" refers to the small things people love about life and how McDonald's fits

---

[35] "McD's CMO Dillon Activates 'The Year of Innovation,'" Interview with Kenneth Hein, *Brand Week*, May 5, 2008, pp. 14-15.

[36] *McDonald's @50*, anniversary book, McDonald's Corporation, 2005, pp. 40-41.

into that life. When asked how long this campaign can last, Neil said, "As far as I can see, and probably beyond that. The campaign is a marvelous idea; the campaign line is clearly one of the most recognized in the world. We believe this to be an asset." This view of campaign endurance is in stark contrast to the previous practice of short-lived campaign ideas. Just look at the following list of McDonald's advertising themes throughout the years:[37]

1960: All American Menu

1961: Look for the Golden Arches

1962: Go for the Goodness at McDonald's

1966: McDonald's... The Closest Thing to Home

1967: McDonald's Is Your Kind of Place

1971: You Deserve a Break Today

1974: McDonald's Sure Is Good to Have Around

1975: We Do It All For You

1976: You, You're the One

1979: Nobody Can Do It Like McDonald's Can

1981: Nobody Makes Your Day Like McDonald's Can

1983: Together, McDonald's and You

1984: It's a Good Time for the Great Taste of McDonald's

1988: Good Time, Great Taste, That's Why This Is My Place

1990: Food, Folks, and Fun

1992: What You Want Is What You Get at McDonald's Today

1995: Have You Had Your Break Today?

1997: My McDonald's

1998: Did Somebody Say McDonald's?

2000: We Love to See You Smile

2002: Smile

2003: i'm lovin' it

---

[37] Ibid.

The Creative Development of "i'm lovin' it"

"i'm lovin' it" became a widely recognized universal expression of how people with a Forever Young spirit feel about life, a spontaneous feeling that we hoped our customers, employees, suppliers, and owner/operators would feel. "ili" crossed cultures, age demographics, and geographies. But, it had to be expressed differently in France, in Australia, in the African-American market, and in the Hispanic-American market.

The McDonald's brand revitalization campaign was much more than advertising. The core idea was developed with a global intent from the beginning. In March 2003, we visited each of our major agencies in our top ten countries around the world. We solicited ideas from everywhere. Each agency had the opportunity to show how it would execute the brand promise with local cultural relevance and global coherence. As a result of the presentations, we identified a common global brand expression that also had relevant local cultural flexibility.

The "i'm lovin' it" idea was born in Unterhaching, Germany. But it was nurtured worldwide. Our view was that to reenergize the brand we needed a whole new brand attitude, not just an advertising campaign. "i'm lovin' it" fit the bill. I was told that this was the first-time ever that McDonald's would be speaking with one voice and a common brand vision around the world. Aligning more than 110 countries worldwide for the first time would not be easy. But because it would meet organizational resistance did not mean we would aim for anything less ambitious. With the support of Jim Cantalupo and Charlie Bell, we overcame this resistance.

It all began with developing relevant consumer insights. This crucial phase of the process—customer insight—began as soon as I arrived. I insisted that we examine everything and truly understand our customers. Here is how we applied some insights to the promotion P.

The Age of I

There is always an opportunity to improve your understanding of a brand and its customer base. To revitalize a brand, we must rebuild brand relevance. The world changes: A static brand loses its place in the customers' mind. So a new brand direction had to be based on a new understanding of our customers and their needs.

The Age of I refers to an era of individuality, inclusivity, and interconnectedness. We saw a generation of people who value their individuality and yet want to belong. This generation wants to be part of a group. They want to be connected to other like-minded individuals. However, they do not want to lose their independence, creativity, and freedom. Although they enjoyed shared values, they also savored their differences.

This understanding informed our new direction. And it brought new insights to our understanding of our own McDonald's brand—a community of individuals. This idea underlies the marketing communications concept we described as brand journalism.

McDonald's is a community of people who share some similar values. It is a global brand that opens its doors where people can feel comfortable under the Golden Arches and maintain their individuality satisfying their individual occasion-based needs.

I-Attitude

Our understanding of the customer indicated that this is a group of people who do not want to be told what to do. They do not want a corporation to tell them what decision to make. This generation wants to think and speak for themselves. The major advertising campaigns that McDonald's had successfully run in the past—"McDonald's is your kind of place," or "You deserve a break today," or "We do it all for you," or "You, You're the One," or "We love to see you smile"—would not ring true with this new generation of consumers. These communications were based on the idea of "us" telling "them" what to do, how to feel, and so on.

Over the years, we told customers that they should take a break today; that we do it all for them; that nobody makes their day like McDonald's; that we would love it if customers would smile; and so on. Cheryl Berman, who was the creative director of the Leo Burnett advertising agency, referred to this approach as a bunch of marketing "We-We." We do this. We do that.

We had to change the way we spoke to our customers from a "we" voice to an "I" voice. We labeled this creative voice the *I-attitude*.

The I-attitude focused on expressing how our customers feel about McDonald's. It expressed how McDonald's fits into their everyday lives. The expression "i'm lovin' it" said that it doesn't matter how old you are, there are things that you love about life and enjoy having McDonald's as a part of your life. The appeal of "i'm lovin' it" is that it did not focus only on product. It portrayed the simple pleasures of everyday life. As McDonald's Canada says on its Web site, McDonald's is "a part of our lives and culture." McDonald's advertising focuses "not only on product, but rather on the overall McDonald's experience, portraying warmth and a real slice of everyday life."

A forever young spirit is not a demographic; it is an attitude about life. Whether people work for McDonald's or visit McDonald's as a guest, the "i'm lovin' it" spirit strikes a relevant chord.

Ideas Don't Care Where They Come From

Great ideas can come from anywhere. We learned this over and over again while developing and executing the "i'm lovin' it" campaign.

One of the greatest strengths of a global brand organization is the extraordinary diversity of creative talent and ideas.

In a global organization, powerful talent is often hidden from view. Great ideas can come from anywhere. Those who say that big companies cannot be creative are wrong. In fact, just the opposite can be true. It is precisely the scale and scope that give a large company an enormous variety of talent on which it can draw.

The problem is that many companies still adhere to the global mantra—"think globally, act locally." The unintended consequence of this kind of thinking is usually, "We will do all the important thinking globally, and you just act without thinking locally." Some people around the world feel the real message is, "Think USA. Do as we say." In fact, some leaders at McDonald's initially resisted the idea that it should adopt a global idea not invented locally.

The challenge for every company, big or small is to leverage the power of ideas. Powerful ideas do not care where they come from. We wanted the best ideas from our communications partners and our suppliers. So we broke down these barriers to creativity.

Along with the fact that the basic, foundational theme of "i'm lovin' it" came from Germany, McDonald's actively sought out and adopted ideas from around the world. We saw what the reimaging of restaurants was doing in France and adapted this concept globally. We saw the success of coffee initiated in Australia, and the coffee opportunity was embraced in a variety of countries.

The new approach to packaging design came from Birmingham, England, and was adopted worldwide—giving McDonald's a global approach to packaging for the first time. While the idea of salads at McDonald's was developed in the United States, the extension of this product into a broader menu concept was developed in Australia. Later this same concept was introduced in Europe. This is a good example of adopt, adapt, and improve.

As well as ideas for food and beverage offerings, there were many other instances of good ideas being created around the world such as a dramatic approach to outdoor advertising initiated in Brazil and later adapted in the United States, Europe, and Asia.

Local creativity was unleashed. New crew T-shirts were designed in the Netherlands that became so desirable these were soon sold in

Dutch department stores. There was a remarkable Toronto, Canada, train station promotion; an impactful pop-up Fruit & Walnut Salad print advertisement from the United States; and eye-catching subway art generated in Taiwan.

Nothing promotes alignment within an organization more than seeing that ideas and creativity from countries other than the home-base country are used around the world.

We learned that communications based on universal truths cross cultural boundaries. For example, some of the advertising developed by DRM for the US Hispanic marketplace was eventually used as general market advertising in several countries. The African-American agency, Burrell, developed effective advertising for McDonald's new premium salads that was used in the general market. A McDonald's global brand commercial reflecting the world's passion for football (soccer in the United States) was created in the United States and produced in Argentina.

Using the brand journalism approach, the marketing behind "i'm lovin' it" shared its common spirit around the world but was implemented locally, customized to address local opportunities.

"i'm lovin' it" became the message integrating McDonald's summer and winter Olympic communications; the World Cup; Justin Timberlake's tour called "Justified and I'm lovin' it;" relationships with Sony, MTV, and ESPN; Internet development; service training; global packaging; event marketing; and the revitalization of Ronald McDonald, just to name a few marketing communications areas.

Packaging

Brand packaging is a critical and remarkable communicator. Everything communicates: signage, letterhead, shopping bags, store design—including in-store aroma and in-store sounds—everything.

When you buy an iPod, before you even get to the object itself, you hold and unpack a glorious, beautifully designed box. When you order from Bliss, the outer box is its signature robin's egg blue box whether it is delivered by the US Post Office, FedEx, or UPS. The distinctive blue Tiffany box is part of the brand promise of a luxury gift. Target's pharmaceutical packaging is a brilliant and socially responsible public statement of its distinctive personality.

Every day millions of people hold the McDonald's brand in their hands. Marketers should not treat packaging as if it were a mere container incidental to the brand: The package is there not only to hold the product, but also to herald the brand. In McDonald's case, there was inconsistency of brand impression. Especially for the McDonald's bag and the cup, it is not just the customer who sees the packaging but those around the customer. With the new package designs, consumers are both holding and promoting the brand in their hand.

Modern day retail packaging in the United States owes a lot to the original Bloomingdale's shopping bag. This bag started a trend but also created unfathomable awareness for the store, helping it to become a fashion icon, the place to shop in the United States during the 1960s.

When you walk in the street holding a Starbucks cup, you are an outdoor advertising medium for the Starbucks brand. Walking around with a Starbucks cup identifies you to others as a coffee connoisseur.

When you are in a meeting and you flip up the cover for your Sony or Apple laptop, the logo reads right side up for your counterpart across the table. The packaging communicates to everyone that this is the brand you prefer.

The woman who bought a McDonald's salad before getting on an airplane holding the package in her hand is communicating to the other passengers that McDonald's is right for her.

We reinvented the McDonald's approach to packaging. Revitalizing the brand meant changing the packaging perspective from viewing packages as merely food and beverage containers to viewing packaging as an effective brand medium with the widest reach. The packaging was given a brand-new look. The global packaging was designed to make a distinctive "i'm lovin' it," "Forever Young" brand statement.

Ronald McDonald

Renovating the image of Ronald McDonald was also an important part of the promotion P. If you have an iconic figure, whether it is Charlie the Tuna, the Geico gecko, the Travelocity gnome, Tony the Tiger, the Aflac Duck, Betty Crocker, the Pillsbury Doughboy, the Marlboro Man, or Mickey Mouse, it is imperative that you treat that brand icon with respect and with the utmost care.

Ronald McDonald is one of the most well-known brand icons. According to reports in *US News & World Report* and *The Economist*, he was the second most recognizable brand icon after Santa Claus.[38] Unfortunately, McDonald's relegated Ronald McDonald to the playpen prison. McDonald's forgot that clowns also appeal to adults. Great clowns like Emmett Kelly's Weary Willie, Charlie Chaplin, and the great mime Marcel Marceau entertained adults. Circus clowns do not just make children smile. The clowns of Cirque du Soleil have broad appeal. But at McDonald's, Ronald McDonald was allowed to be positioned only as entertainment for kids.

As mentioned previously, Ray Kroc designed McDonald's to be a happy place, and Ronald McDonald became the personified icon of that happiness. His role was to create happiness. So to revitalize the McDonald's brand we had to revitalize Ronald McDonald's role.

The importance of having a brand promise is played out in the redefinition of Ronald McDonald. All we had to do was give him a contemporary, "Forever Young" spirit in ways that appealed to more than just children.

Redefinition was not new for Ronald McDonald. McDonald's had changed him before, albeit not always for the good. Some changes were small, some were big, but they were changes nevertheless.

---

[38] Spake, Amanda, "How McNuggets changed the world," *US News & World Report*, January 22, 2001; "Did somebody say a loss?" *The Economist*, April 12, 2003.

The Story of Ronald McDonald

Originally, Ronald McDonald had a sort of "home-made look"—the "you-can-do-this-yourself-at-home, folks" feel about him; all you needed was a paper cup and a wig.

In the late 1960s, Ronald McDonald became more active, and he was even given his very own Flying Hamburger Vehicle. As part of his "aviation" persona, he landed at a McDonald's in an American Airlines jet.

In the 1970s, Ronald McDonald went through a number of changes. The shape of his pockets changed from food containers to regular large-size pockets. He wore shoes of different colors, blue and yellow, not only red. And, he was located in a special place called McDonald's Land.

In 1973, McDonald's restyled his wig with a more tousled look and a side part. His makeup was modified—all this in an effort to make him look more au courant with the swinging '70s.

In 1974, Ronald McDonald became physically more acrobatic and socially conscious. This was the year of the first Ronald McDonald House for the families of critically ill children.

In 1975, Ronald McDonald's appearance changed again, returning to his pre-1974 look. His eyebrows were aligned and his wig became smoother and rounder. The bottom pockets were no longer aligned, and his pants legs were less baggy.

But in the early 1980s, changes to Ronald McDonald went beyond just wardrobe. Ronald McDonald became a cowboy. Perhaps you remember "Ronald McDonald on the Cheeseburger McTrail"? He was also a Viking and an astronaut. He had almost as many careers as Barbie!

As time went on, Ronald McDonald evolved to a less heroic kind of clown, one with more visual humor and a touch of magic. But it had become magic for kids; Ronald McDonald became a small child's magical friend.

Revitalization of Ronald

McDonald's made a mistake keeping Ronald McDonald in kindergarten. But we realized that it is never too late. Cheryl Berman of Leo Burnett led the charge to revitalize Ronald McDonald. She saw a way to broaden his image so that he would appeal not just to children, but also to everyone with a "Forever Young" spirit. She and her team believed passionately that Ronald was a great communicator and empathizer. Ronald McDonald loves life and knows that there is a lot of lovin' in all of us. He could help McDonald's express the warm and friendly feeling that "life is like McDonald's and i'm lovin' it."

We knew that Ronald McDonald was a terrific ambassador for the brand. Charlie Bell promoted Ronald to McDonald's Chief Happiness Officer. We decided that Ronald McDonald would appear in some of the Olympics advertising; he met and had fun with sports stars such as Yao Ming, Serena Williams, and Venus Williams. Ronald McDonald's wardrobe was expanded to include seven new outfits in his signature color scheme.

Everything Ronald McDonald did would be on behalf of elevating the brand to higher and higher levels in line with the brand promise appealing to all those who have a "Forever Young" attitude.

But, we also recognized that Ronald McDonald could be an important ambassador encouraging kids to both eat better and be more active. Ronald McDonald has played this educational role before. For example, he encouraged kids to fasten their safety belts. He could play this valuable role again.

The Ronald McDonald School Show was changed to encourage children to eat right and participate in more fun activities to get the body moving. The Nordic countries created a Happy Mile Program making the connection between the Happy Meal and physical activity. Around the world, McDonald's created school programs to encourage children to eat right and be active.

It is easy to focus just on encouraging physical activity. This will be perceived as just a way to shift the burden of responsibility from McDonald's to the parent and the child. But, there is a shared responsibility.

It was important to have a proper balance in these communications. The primary focus of a food company needs to be on the food. The food we eat makes a difference. McDonald's has a responsibility to provide healthful choices and also a responsibility to encourage people to make better choices. Encouraging kids to eat right is important.

Ronald McDonald could help. For example, as noted, McDonald's provided milk as a beverage alternative. But, when a new child-friendly package was introduced with Ronald McDonald on the package, sales increased dramatically.

Conclusion

Revitalization of a brand is a challenging task. It requires commitment to the brand purpose and brand promise. It requires willingness to change belief systems and practices. It requires the ability to reject outdated views of marketing. And more important, it requires leadership. McDonald's had that leadership with Jim Cantalupo and Charlie Bell as the architects of the Plan to Win.

When a brand becomes so successful that no one wants to risk a change, it is committing brand suicide. Remember that avoiding change, accepting complacency, and resting on your laurels is a formula for eventual failure. Brand consultant Martin Lindstrom says that, "Brands need to grow with their customers and pay heed to their ever-changing needs—whatever those needs may be."[39] What got a

---

[39] *McDonald's @50*, anniversary book, Martin Lindstrom page, McDonald's Corporation, 2005, p.247.

brand to where it is today may not get the brand to where it needs to go tomorrow. You need to know what to keep and what to change.

All companies must regularly reexamine their business practices and their brands. In a dynamic and complex world staying with successful past approaches may not yield tomorrow's superior results.

The Do's and Don'ts of Reinventing the Brand Experience

Do

- **Be willing to abandon practices that do not yield the results you want**—Just because you have done something one way for years (and it has been successful for you) does not mean that it will continue to be a successful approach.

- **Take a multidimensional approach to marketing**—Today's world is more fragmented and complex than ever. People have many sides and dimensions. A young adult female can also be a mother, a friend, and an employee. Take into account the many-me's of me.

- **Use the multisegment approach**—All the five action Ps are affected. Keep this in mind as you develop service initiatives, new products, place redesign, pricing strategies, and promotion components including advertising, packaging, cultural marketing, and the care of your icons. Remember you are reinventing across all the five action Ps.

- **Make sure that your service plans and programs reinforce the brand**—Service is more than just serving the customer. Employees need to know that they are making a difference, no matter how small.

- **Respect your employees**—Treat them well; teach them well. They are ambassadors for the brand.

- **Instill pride**—Allow your employees to be proud out loud. Your benchmark should be an employee recommending to a friend that he or she should work for your organization. In marketing, having pride is not a deadly sin; it is deadly not having pride.

- **Create an "on-board" experience for every employee**—Make the first impression count. For each new employee, impart something about the brand on the first day. It will begin to instill pride at once.

- **Offer skills for a lifetime**—People today do not seem to be looking for that lifetime job. Instead they want to gain skills that have value over the course of their life.

- **Gain commitment from all levels of management**—Break the middle and upper management bottleneck of resistance to branding and new ideas. All your efforts will be for nothing if employees have managers who are stuck in the business as usual pattern.

- **Focus on increasing frequency and penetration**—Both matter. This is not an either-or discussion. You must attract new customers *and* make sure that current customers continue to visit.

- **Put customers at the beginning of the innovation process**—Innovations must address expressed customer needs, unarticulated needs, and future unmet needs.

- **Know what defines all the places of your brand**—Just because you do not own restaurants or retail establishments does not mean your brand can skip the "place" P. Your place may be the Internet or the phone call to your 800 number.

- **Focus on both parts of the value equation**—A focus on only one half of the equation will not help to increase perceived customer value.

- **Base price decisions on the customer's perceived value rather than on cost**—Fully understand and correctly judge the effects of price manipulations.

- **Remind people that you have a (wide) range of prices**—Be sure that your offers are perceived to be fairly priced.

- **Create a communications program that promotes the brand**—Every communication must enhance the brand, raising it to a higher level of appeal to and affinity with the customer.

- **Practice brand journalism**—Multidimensional customers deserve multidimensional communications. Simplifying a brand to a single word is not simplification, it is simplistic. Simplistic marketing is marketing suicide. Brands are complex.

- **Practice cultural marketing**—Brands are multidimensional and cross borders. In today's world, people are affected by all sorts of geographic influences. Take advantage of these as long as they enhance your brand's promised experience.

- **Review your packaging**—Boxes are banners for your brand. No matter how small or how big, your package communicates. Make sure the package communicates the right things about your brand.

- **Reexamine your icons**—Make sure that you are treating your icons with care and respect. Make sure the icon is not stuck in the past someplace. You can revitalize an icon without relinquishing its heritage and core values.

- **Be proud of your products**—Employees should respect and use your products. It doesn't make sense to have employees who do not think the products you sell are "good enough" for them. Make sure that product changes are "added value" not "incremental degradation."

Don't

- **Don't launch external campaigns before you announce initiatives internally**—Your people come first. If you launch an initiative externally your people will believe they are second-place citizens. And, your customers will suffer too. Customers will have expectations that your employees will not meet because they have not yet been informed and/or trained.

- **Don't allow middle and senior managers to thwart your efforts among employees**—The bottleneck in the middle can deter any new efforts to gain traction within an organization. Business as usual will defeat your educational efforts every time. Make sure all levels of management are exposed to new initiatives in manners that are appropriate to the activities of their respective jobs.

- **Don't abandon your core principles or products**—Just because you have a new initiative or a new segment does not mean you should jettison your history or core products. Renovation may be in order: Think Tide, new and improved more than 50 times. Different ingredients may be required (such as substitutes for trans fats or sugar). Falling in love with a new product should not be a detriment to your existing product.

- **Don't practice denominator marketing**—Price and value are not the same thing. Denominator marketing will eventually position you in a commodity corner.

- **Don't focus communications solely on the price**—Selling the deal instead of selling the brand cheapens the brand. Focus on "great brand at a great price" rather than just "great price."

- **Don't define promotion as tactical individual activities**—Everything communicates. Promotion means elevating the perception of the brand. So, promotion is not just advertising and not just a series of individual sales-driving activities. If it is associated with the brand, it should improve the perception of the brand.

- **Don't become complacent**—Thinking that what was successful in the past will necessarily continue to work in the future is riskier than making a change.

6

Rule #4: Reinforce a Results Culture

Creating a results culture means creating a culture that is evaluated based on producing measurable results. This means defining measurable milestones and rewarding people based on performance.

There are three rules-based practices for creating a results culture:

- Identify measurable milestones
- Implement recognition and rewards
- Initiate the Balanced Brand-Business Scorecard

McDonald's was not a results culture. Brand image declined, same-store sales declined, profits declined, and share price declined. Yet there was little correlation between executive rewards and business performance. Even though McDonald's business performance was deteriorating, top management continued to be rewarded. This made no sense; management rewards need to be placed in line with brand and business goals and shareholder interests.

People manage what management measures, recognizes, and rewards. We need to create a Balanced Brand-Business Scorecard that evaluates whether we are producing the right results the right way.

Rich Floersch, head of human resources and the team leader of the People P, redesigned the management evaluation system. Performance, against both business and marketing metrics, were increasingly correlated with salaries and bonuses.

All Growth Is Not Equally Valuable

There is high-quality growth and low-quality growth. Low-quality growth actually destroys value even while revenues increase. Managing for growth is not enough. We must manage for quality revenue growth. Creating brand value is the basis for quality revenue growth. Quality revenue growth is the basis for enduring profitable growth. Enduring profitable growth is how we create sustainable increases in shareholder value. The Balanced Brand-Business Scorecard measures how well we are doing.

To create brand value, marketers must evolve their thinking from product management to brand management, from supply-driven management to customer-driven management, from "how can we do it cheaper" to "how can we do it better." The McDonald's growth goal changed from being bigger, to being bigger by being better.

Penetration and Frequency

This discussion has been going on for decades: Which is more important for my brand, generating more customers or creating more brand loyalty?

Both are critical measures for any brand. *Penetration* refers to having more customers. Growing the customer base is important. *Brand loyalty* refers to having customers purchase more often, building brand preference and reducing price sensitivity.

The bottom-line objective needs to be the combination of more customers, more often, more brand loyal, and more profitable.

When I arrived in September 2002, the McDonald's customer base per store was decreasing. If this trend were allowed to continue, the end game would have to be that the last customer would have to visit McDonald's 50 million times per day just to maintain McDonald's volume!

It is possible to have increased brand loyalty among a shrinking base of customers. But increasing loyalty among fewer customers is a risky business. Jaguar found this out as its customer base dwindled.

The ongoing brand challenge is to continuously attract customers and to create a positive experience so that they return and are more loyal. This means creating and reinforcing an enduring and profitable bond between a customer and a brand. We cannot build a successful brand focusing only on customer attraction. Attracting new customers who do not return is a fool's errand. But, relying on repeat customers within a declining customer base is also risky.

When it comes to the bottom-line brand-business goals, our goals are to attract more customers with greater frequency and increased brand loyalty and with increased profitability.

Four Drivers of Customer Value

The first step in building a results culture is to define measurable milestones. Managing for value begins with strategy and ends with business results. We must measure sales and profitability. We must measure and monitor changes in brand reputation. To be a market leader, you need sales volume. To be a profitable market leader, you need brand loyalty.

Of course, the first step is to be efficient. This means reducing costs by eliminating waste, increasing productivity of the available resources, and optimizing allocation of limited resources. This relates to financial discipline and operational excellence.

McDonald's was not getting a satisfactory return on incremental invested capital. Matt Paull introduced a more disciplined approach that yielded significant improvements in *ROIIC* (*Return on Incremental Invested Capital*).

Improving productivity alone is not really a strategy for enduring prosperity. The only way to enduring profitable growth is by achieving a sustainable competitive advantage that increases sales and margins.

To be enduring, we must build both the sales and profitability of the brand, and we must also continuously strengthen the brand. The brand must be powerful. Brand power is built along three dimensions: familiar identity, relevant differentiation, and authority (quality, leadership, and trust).

A powerful brand is not the same as a big brand. And repeat purchase is not necessarily a sign of brand loyalty. It is a mistake to assume that repeat behavior is an indication of brand loyalty. Non-loyal repeat purchase is a threat to brand value. Educating a generation of customers to repeat only because of price and convenience does not build brand value; it destroys brand value.

Cable television is a good example of how having repeat customers does not necessarily mean having loyal customers. When cable television was the only alternative, people joined. But the service and responsiveness of the operators was terrible. People felt trapped. When the availability of small, easy-to-install satellite dishes became widespread, frustrated customers flocked to dish networks, abandoning cable TV.

Airline frequency programs based on mileage rewards do not necessarily build brand loyalty. They do reward frequent travelers. But there are those who may fly Northwest Airlines frequently to Detroit. This does not necessarily mean that these frequent travelers would rate Northwest as their favorite airline.

McDonald's fell into the frequency-loyalty trap. Frequency is not necessarily the same as loyalty. The majority of McDonald's most frequent customers were not loyal to the McDonald's brand. McDonald's most valuable customers did not have a favorable view of the McDonald's brand.[1] Brand loyalty is more than repeat purchase. Brand loyalty is repeat purchase based on a commitment to the brand. This means that your customers believe that your brand is the superior alternative for satisfying their particular need in a particular

---

[1] Light, Larry, speech to the Association of National Advertisers, October 2004.

context. It means that your brand is their favorite—the brand they prefer, the brand they intend to buy again, the brand they are willing to recommend.

The result was that McDonald's became increasingly vulnerable to competitive offers.

Brand Loyalty

Building sales volume is important. For enduring profitable growth, we must not only build the quantity of sales, we must also build the quality of our sales, and we must align the culture around building both quantity and quality of sales. This means ridding the culture of a "sales is all that matters" mentality and instilling into the culture the concept of building sales based on brand loyalty.

At McDonald's, we recognized that it is not enough to have customers frequent the brand. We wanted people to frequent the brand because they favored the brand. As the McDonald's brand purpose stated, the goal is "to be our customers' favorite place and way to eat."[2] McDonald's led the market in penetration and frequency. But, frequent customers did not favor McDonald's. They frequented McDonald's because it was convenient and low-priced.

Brand Loyalty and Durable Goods

The concept of loyalty to the brand, not just to the product or service is particularly important in durable goods. In durable goods, if you wait for your customer to buy another refrigerator, for example, you may wait for 10 to 15 years or more. Having other products with the same brand name that a customer can buy more frequently increases that customer's familiarity with the brand and the customer's perception of the brand authority and specialness. Samsung, LG, and Sony have used this strategy with great success.

---

[2] McDonald's 2005 Annual Report, p. 10.

Brand Loyalty Ladder

Brand loyalty is like a ladder: There are degrees of commitment to a brand, from minimal to real commitment—steps you take to go to higher levels of brand commitment. The process of revitalization requires that we understand and audit the entire pool of users to determine where the potential customers are and how these customers array themselves on the loyalty ladder.

In the universe of potential customers, there are those who are simply unfamiliar with the brand. Among those customers who are familiar, there are two main groups: those who are not using the brand and those who are, to some degree.

Among those who are not using the brand, there are customers who:

- Have not tried the brand
- Have tried the brand but have not rejected the brand
- Have tried and rejected the brand

In 2002, there was a growing number of people familiar with the McDonald's brand. These people had experienced the brand in the past, had fond memories of the brand, but were not current users even though they were not rejecting the brand. This was a fertile area for brand revitalization. We needed to understand how to win these customers back to the brand.

In general, when analyzing a brand's customers, among those who are using the brand to some degree, there are four types of brand commitment (see Figure 6.1):

- **Commodity consideration**—Brands in this group are in a customer's consideration set. These brands are perceived to be basically the same. Consumers like the category, but they do not see relevant brand differences. Price and convenience are the differentiators.
- **Short list**—These brands are on the customer's short list, usually the customer's top three favorite brands.

- **Preference**—A preferred brand is the one that the customer prefers above the others, their favorite choice.
- **Enthusiasm**—Brands in this category are ones the customer prefers to buy even when their second choice brand costs less. These customers not only intend to repeat, they intend to recommend the brand to their friends.

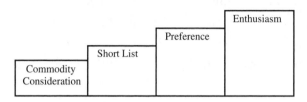

Figure 6.1   Brand Loyalty Ladder

Building brand favoritism means moving people up this loyalty ladder. The goal is to increase the number of customers who not only prefer your brand but also prefer the brand even though there is a price premium. These enthusiasts not only intend to continue to buy the brand, they would recommend it to a friend.

Balanced Brand-Business Scorecard

A Balanced Brand-Business Scorecard needs to be created. Metrics to evaluate performance on each action P were defined. Key measures such as store cleanliness, brand loyalty, and so on were standardized providing a globally consistent view of progress.

At McDonald's, the milestones were published for everyone to see. Quarterly meetings with area executives throughout the year focused on reviewing performance against the milestones. The scorecards were displayed prominently in Charlie's office. He had a wall-size board specifically made to display the brand's progress. The Balanced Brand-Business Scorecard was designed to assure that while it is good to produce the right results, it is important to produce the right results the right way. The McDonald's Brand Scorecard included measures relating to each of the five action Ps, customer perceptions of the brand, as well as mystery shopper scores.

"Every job in McDonald's is dependent on those consumers coming into our store at the front counter. And that's what causes everything else in McDonald's. And without those people, we wouldn't be here."[3]

The fundamental goal of business is value creation, but Ray Kroc understood that to create value for investors, we must create value for customers. Ray knew that all cash flow begins with a customer exchanging money for your offer. The business has little value unless there is value to customers.

Brand power and brand loyalty are measurable. A brand's image is measurable, and the brand's value is measurable. A Balanced Brand-Business Scorecard takes into account these performance indicators as well as the brand's sales, share, and profits.

Think of the scorecard as a dashboard; it has all the critical elements for driving your brand on the road of enduring profitable growth (see Figure 6.2).

Sales/Share	Profit
Brand Power	Brand Image
Brand Loyalty Ladder	Brand Value

Figure 6.2   Plan to Win: Brand Dashboard

Revitalizing a brand requires an organization that is committed to measuring the results of our progress toward achievement of our Plan to Win. All the activities and all the articulations of where we want to be and how we plan to get there are irrelevant if we do not institute a

---

[3] Kroc, Ray, TV interview with Tom Snyder, *Tomorrow*, 1977.

yardstick for assessing movement. It aligns the organization on increasing the value of the brand.

Regardless of how glorious the philosophy is and inspirational the words are, most managers will overlook something that is not measured and rewarded.

McDonald's Plan to Win Milestones

It is essential to put in place and implement a corporatewide measurement program; otherwise, it is just an academic exercise. McDonald's aligned all business units around the same goals. Just as it had common financial measures, McDonald's instituted common business measures across all aspects of the business—the tangibles and intangibles—as articulated in the Plan to Win.

McDonald's created customer-based measures for each of the five action Ps: people, product, place, price, and promotion. And for each of these five action Ps, McDonald's created three-year milestones.

Examples for the people P were measures for key service criteria, employee commitment, and employer reputation. The measures for product focused on those that would help define favorite food and beverage. For place, the measures included items such as cleanliness and other items relating to the image of the store. For the price P, value for money was an important measure. And for promotion advertising, effectiveness and brand trust were assessed.[4]

There were global measures and local measures. In addition, a quality improvement program was instituted to evaluate local store performance.[5] This comprehensive restaurant review program was led by the persistence of Mike Roberts, McDonald's US president at the time. Mystery shoppers evaluated each store regularly. The purpose of the Restaurant Operations Improvement Program (ROIP) was to help

---

[4] McDonald's Shareholders Brochure, October 2003.
[5] McDonald's Corporate Responsibility Report, 2004.

operators and managers identify shortcomings and help them improve performance by providing the necessary tools and training. The ROIP "involves evaluations related to 12 areas (or 'systems') that directly impact customer experience and, hence, business results."[6]

Putting a system like this into place takes patience and courage. It is a lot easier to describe than to actually do. Gaining agreement on common performance measures is an accomplishment in any organization. It is a particular accomplishment in decentralized global organizations where geographies have different standard measures in place. There is resistance to changing measures. Time and again, McDonald's was confronted with the complaint that a new common system will invalidate the years of normative data collected locally.

McDonald's Measurable Milestones[7]

- **People**—Measures include increases in speed of service and friendliness scores and a reduction in service-related complaints.

- **Product**—Measures include improvements in hot and fresh food scores.

- **Place**—Measures include a return to an all-time high in cleanliness scores.

- **Price**—Measures include improvement in value for money scores and restaurant margins.

- **Promotion**—Measures include increased brand awareness and a return to the all-time high in Happy Meal units per restaurant.

A Balanced Brand-Business Scorecard assesses progress against a vision of brand perfection. In other words, it is not just about reaching achievable objectives; we also need to evaluate whether we are making

---

[6] Ibid.

[7] "McDonald's Revitalization Plan," brochure for shareholders, *McDonald's Corporation*, October 29, 2003.

progress toward our ultimate goals. This means we must incorporate the brand vision into our measures. We compare where we are versus where we want to be in the future. Are we making progress toward the defined brand destination? How close, or far, are we from our stated goals?

For example, some companies measure customer satisfaction versus what they consider to be an achievable objective such as 80% customer satisfaction. But Toyota aims for zero defects and 100% customer satisfaction. These may not be achievable next year, but Toyota measures whether they are making progress toward goals such as these. Those who measure achievement compared to achievable objectives will lose to those who set higher goals, measuring progress toward a vision of perfection.

Brand Equity

It is commonly recognized that the value of a brand is among a company's most valuable assets. So, measuring progress in building brand equity can be a useful measure of our effectiveness as marketers.

GM Versus Toyota

If you want to truly appreciate the financial value of a brand, think about the Toyota Corolla and Geo Prism, automobiles manufactured in the late '80s at a common production facility in California called NUMMI. Both vehicles were manufactured on the same line, by the same employees, and to the same quality standards. Because of the differential power of the Toyota brand, the Corolla not only cost $300 more, but it also sold better. This yielded $108 million for Toyota and $128 million more for Toyota dealers. The makers of the Geo Prism concluded from this experience that they could not make money in this particular market segment and discontinued the brand. As history bears out, the difference was not the production process nor the people who produced the vehicle. The difference was the value of the respective brands. That brand value was worth millions of dollars.

Brand equity is the customer's perception of the financial worth of the brand identity. It is the difference in the financial value of a branded good or service compared to an equivalent good or service without the brand identity. As Ray Kroc once said, "A hamburger patty is a piece of meat. But a McDonald's hamburger is a piece of meat with character."[8]

Brands do not always add value. Sometimes they subtract value. When Carlos Ghosn came to Nissan, he was quoted in the press on the perceived value of the Nissan brand. Based on recent research, he said, "Compared to an equivalent Toyota vehicle, Nissan vehicles in North America are worth about $1,000 less."[9] In other words, the Nissan brand subtracted $1,000 per vehicle perceived value.

McDonald's Coffee Versus Starbucks Coffee

In its March 2007 issue, *Consumer Reports* reported on its coffee taste tests. Trained tasters went to McDonald's, Starbucks, Dunkin' Donuts, and Burger King. The headline of this taste comparison was that McDonald's coffee tastes better and costs less than coffee from Starbucks, Burger King, and Dunkin' Donuts. "We compared the rivals with Starbucks, all in basic black—no flavors, milk, or sugar—and you know what? McDonald's bested the rest." The magazine said that "McDonald's coffee was decent and moderately strong" while Starbucks coffee was "strong, but burnt and bitter enough to make your eyes water."

Most consumers, however, pay attention to the brand experience. That is why you find people paying more for a Starbucks coffee versus a McDonald's coffee.

It is not enough to measure marketing success through increases in market share. Market share can be bought through bribes, or through brand exploitation. For instance, in the automotive world, these are

---

[8] Kroc, Ray, with Anderson, Robert, *Grinding It Out*, St. Martin's Paperback ed., p. 102.
[9] Thorton, Emily, with bureau reports, "Remaking Nissan," *BusinessWeek International*, November 15, 1999.

called incentives, zero percent down, or $2,500 off the MSRP. For McDonald's, this meant excessive dependence on price promotion.

But brand value must be earned and re-earned. It is possible to have a brand whose sales go up, but its value goes down. Some companies wonder why sales are up but business is so bad. These companies wonder why with increasing revenues, margins are down.

The concept of brand power and its relationship to brand value is more than just nice marketing phraseology. There is real, genuine bottom-line impact. As brand power goes up, price sensitivity goes down, and sales and profitability increase.

Price Elasticity

Price elasticity is a useful indicator of brand equity. We learned from basic economics that as price goes up, demand goes down. Economists call it demand instead of volume because actual volume depends on your distribution, promotional activities, and a variety of things. This price-demand equation is quantifiable.

Here is an example. Imagine that we plot brand demand against price for a particular brand. The chart would look like Figure 6.3.

Now, imagine that we have also calculated the same line for the major competitive alternative. From this analysis, we can determine the *brand value differential* (see Figure 6.4).

Brand B has greater customer perceived value than Brand A. Consumers are willing to pay a higher price for this brand. Or, at the same price, demand will be higher for this brand. In other words, the brand on the right has a significant brand value strategic advantage.

Brand value differential is defined as the price difference that would yield equal demand for the two brands. In other words, at what prices would the average consumer in the selected market segment consider the two brands to be equal in value. Brand A has a significant brand value disadvantage.

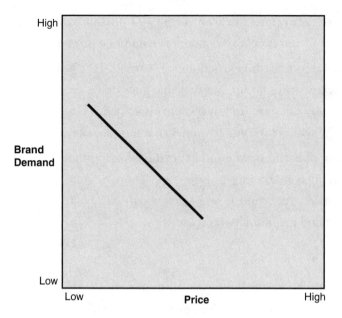

Figure 6.3   Price elasticity

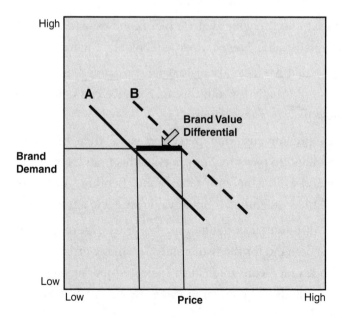

Figure 6.4   Brand value differentiation

In one case, for a technical product priced on the average around $2,000, one brand had a brand value advantage of more than $300. In the case of Nissan, as just mentioned, Carlos Ghosn reported that Nissan had a brand value disadvantage in North America of around $1,000 relative to Toyota.[10]

We worked with a consumer durable product priced at around $1,000. The brand had a negative brand value differential of about $200. The result was that without heavy discounting versus major competitors, this brand would lose significant share.

A business-to business service client had a brand value differential advantage of $43 per transaction over its major competitors. This kind of advantage is a major contributor toward superior brand profitability.

Just because you have a brand value advantage does not mean you should charge the highest prices that you can. That is a strategic decision that depends on whether the plan is to maintain share, grow share, or exploit the brand.

Sometimes marketers are tempted to maximize short-term profitability of the next transaction, sacrificing long-term value creation. You cannot continue to raise prices to make up for lack of volume. It was related to me that Ray Kroc liked to emphasize the point that raising prices without justification is a sad way to run a business. He understood the concept of "fair value."

A study by Boulding, Lee, and Staelin concluded that "brand-focused communications decrease price elasticity."[11] Overemphasis on price—whether in a promotional vehicle or in a promotional ad destroys rather than builds brand loyalty. These types of price

---

[10] Ibid.

[11] Boulding, W., Lee, E., Staelin, R., "The Long-Term Differentiation Value of Marketing Communication Actions," *MSI*, Working Paper, 1994, 92-134.

communications hurt brand equity. If the emphasis of the marketing message is price, then brand loyalty is being exploited, not enhanced.[12]

A high-tech product marketer included the brand value differential measure as part of the reward system for brand management. The fair value analysis and the brand value differential can be used as measures of the brand management progress in creating customer-perceived value.

Management of Progress

Creating a Balanced Brand-Business Scorecard not only allows for measurement of progress but also management of progress.

At McDonald's, we used the Balanced Brand-Business Scorecard for assessing the health of the brand around the world and for evaluating the progress we were making toward our overall brand destination of becoming our customer's favorite place and way to eat. We also used the scorecard as a resource to guide priorities for continuous improvement. Where are the successes? Where are the problems? What is working? Why? What is not working? Why? Where should we allocate resources?[13]

The goal of a Balanced Brand-Business Scorecard is ultimately to help create a learning organization—not just to learn what progress we are making, but also to learn how to improve.

The leadership of Eric Leinenger and Jerry Calabrese turned the Balanced Brand-Business Scorecard into a useful learning tool. A remarkably user-friendly database was created to enable a variety of customized analyses to learn how to improve. A valuable part of their

---

[12] Light, Larry, with Morgan, Richard, *The Fourth Wave: Brand Loyalty Marketing*, The Coalition for Brand Equity, American Association of Advertising Agencies, NY, 1994.

[13] The measurement goals are articulated in the Shareholders Brochure, October 2003, pp. 4-6.

contribution was creating simple analytics to highlight where the brand is performing well and on what attributes it is underperforming. Continuous improvement is the management priority.

Management of progress needs to include learning how to make progress. Learning from each other is the best way to continue to improve our performance. Global learning is based on three principles:

- *Adopt* an idea that seems to be working somewhere else.
- *Adapt* that idea to the local market environment.
- Continuously *improve* the idea.

A properly designed Balanced Brand-Business Scorecard provides important learning, from successes and from failures. Having a shared measurement system does not just aim to recognize and reward, it helps to spur ideas as well as prevent us from repeating failed ideas.

Creating a results culture sometimes leads to excessive reliance just on the reported measures. We should measure all that we can measure. But there is no substitute for good judgment. We must be able to weigh the results against the knowledge and judgment that we possess and make the decisions that need to be made. Waiting for the right research number only keeps you and the company waiting. Waiting for just the right answer sometimes causes us to interpret the results in a way that reinforces what we are hoping to find. Data does not make decisions. People do.

The Do's and Don'ts of Creating a Results Culture

Do

- **Focus the organization around brand value**—To be the best value, you cannot compete on price alone. You cannot cost manage your way to enduring profitable growth. Galvanize the organization around the value equation.

- **Build brand power**—Powerful brands make money. The goal must be to become the identity that is most familiar, the highest quality, and most trustworthy source of a relevant, differentiated promised experience. Remember to focus on the four components of a powerful brand: identity, familiarity, specialness, and authority.

- **Grow brand loyalty**—Move your customers up the loyalty ladder. Take care of your most loyal customers.

- **Understand your rejectors**—Know why people have problems with you; know why they are turning away. These may be bigger issues than you realize. You may be able to win these people back along with others as well. We had one client who was stunned to learn that consumers had more than 500 problems within his product category even though his particular company continued to make product changes every year.

- **Measure what you want managed**—Measure more than just sales, share growth, and profit growth. Build both quantity of share and quality of share simultaneously.

- **Align around the measures**—Use the metrics not just to evaluate progress but to manage progress as well. Don't punish low scores but learn from them. Reward performance.

- **Conduct key research**—Many different types of research can contribute data.

Don't

- **Don't misinterpret results**—Accept the results and move forward. This means analyze, interpret, and synthesize but do not manipulate.

- **Don't rely on the results/data to decide for you**—Data does not decide. You are the "decider." You are the decision-maker. Use the data to understand and prioritize the decisions that need to be made. Don't get bogged down with the paralysis of analysis.

- **Don't use results to support preconceived opinions**—Results and data are opinion neutral. Imposing your preconceived notions on the data may point people and resources in the wrong direction.

7

Rule #5: Rebuild Brand Trust

A powerful brand is more than a trademark. A powerful brand is a trustmark. Trust is an important prerequisite for building long-term brand loyalty. Trustworthiness is a key component of brand power. Without trust, there can be no brand loyalty.

When you trust a brand, you become committed to it. Trust is the most important prerequisite for building long-term brand loyalty. Trust facilitates persuasion. Trust facilitates the acceptance of new information. Trust is a relationship criterion more than a transaction criterion.

How do we define trust? Trust is "a generalized expectancy held by an individual or group that the word, promise, verbal or written statement of another individual or group can be relied upon."[1] We define brand trust as the "generalized expectation that the promise of a brand can be relied upon."

Trust cannot be bought. It must be earned and re-earned. It accumulates over time. It is lasting, but when damaged, the bond can break quickly. It can take years to build and be lost overnight. Trust is a necessary ingredient for long-term commitment. And once a brand bond is strengthened, it is difficult to break. When it does break, however, it can break with suddenness. Although trust is a valued prize that takes time to build and adds to the bottom line, it can be easily violated.

---

[1] Rotter, J. B., "Generalized Expectancies for Interpersonal Trust," *American Psychology*, vol. 26, 1971, 443-452.

For example, trust is key in the consumption of bottled water: We assume there are no chemicals, lead, poisons, toxins, and so on. Perrier had a brand trust advantage that it quickly lost in the early 1990s.

In February 1990, Perrier, the brand that made bottled mineral water chic, was forced to recall its bottled water in the United States after tests showed the water contained benzene. Initially, Perrier did not respond except for the recall. Perrier did not see the issue as a global one. Perrier did not provide a consistent response nor did it coordinate messages to the public. The result was a confused and concerned consumer. What could happen to me as a daily drinker of Perrier? Initially no answers were provided, and when the answers came, they were not consistent depending on geography.

The brand was reintroduced later that year, but another problem soon arose. A claim made on the bottle's label was proven to be false and raised the issues of truthfulness and trustworthiness with consumers.[2] Eventually, in 1992, the brand was sold to Nestle. However, the brand never did regain its pre-1990 market share, and today faces a whole host of rivals.[3]

A consumer may try a new, unfamiliar brand out of curiosity, or because of an exceptional price offer. But if your goal is brand loyalty, you must build trust.

Today, trust is an increasingly important challenge. When things are uncertain, people look for touchstones of trust. Trust is comforting. Trust minimizes perceived risk. Trust facilitates persuasion. It eases the acceptance of new information. People are more willing to

---

[2] The Perrier bottle indicated that the water came directly from the natural spring and went into the green bottle. As it turned out, the "gas" to make the bubbles was added after the water came out of the spring. Perrier had to change its label to indicate the addition of "gas" in the bottling plant.

[3] James, George, "Perrier Recalls Its Water in U.S. After Benzene is Found in Bottles," *The New York Times*, February 10, 1990; see also, Haig, Matt, *Brand Failures: The Truth About the 100 Biggest Branding Mistakes of All Time*, London: Kogan Page Ltd., 2003, 129-131.

accept a line extension from a brand they trust. Trust contributes to creating an enduring brand relationship.

The practice for rebuilding trust is extremely challenging. Leadership must focus on evaluating both internal and external commitment and behavior. This was critical for revitalizing the McDonald's brand.

At our consulting firm, Arcature LLC, we have a four-point approach to internal marketing, which is discussed in this chapter.

Crisis of Credibility

Customers are not only more knowledgeable, demanding, quality conscious, and value conscious, they are also more skeptical, more questioning, and far less trusting. There appears to be an "antitrust" movement in the making.

There have been some visible trust-erosion cases—Enron, for example, or Firestone tires on Ford SUVs. As Sophocles once wrote: "When trust dies, mistrust blossoms."[4] Trust is under attack. People are losing trust in political leadership, public education, religious leaders, business, and so on.

Rebuilding trust is critical. Al Golin, Ray Kroc's public relations man, says in his book, *Trust or Consequences*, that "To build a brand, trust has to be an integral part of any strategy." He says that trust is "the great intangible at the heart of truly long-term success."[5] For enduring brand loyalty to exist, trust must exist.

Trust can be an enormous asset. Brands such as Johnson & Johnson, Whole Foods, H&M, Nordstrom, In-N-Out Burger, Amazon, eBay, and Procter & Gamble that have the deep, lasting trust of their customers have a huge advantage over their competition.

---

[4] Sophocles, *Oedipus Colonus*, 1.611.
[5] Golin, Al, *Trust or Consequences: Build Trust Today or Lose Your Market Tomorrow*, New York: AMACON, 2003.

Rebuilding trust is an important component of brand revitalization. The importance of building trust is just common sense. But it is also true that in many instances, common sense is not common in brand management.

Five Principles of Trust Building

To help the revitalization of a brand, here are five trust-building principles:

- You are what you do.
- Lead the debate; don't hide from it.
- Openness is an opportunity.
- Trustworthy messages must come from a trustworthy source.
- Be a good citizen.

You Are What You Do

Trust must be displayed before it can be declared. Customers must consider your brand worthy of trust before they commit to trusting your brand. Saying "trust me" does not track with today's customers.

Yet, marketers use the "trust me" approach as often as politicians. In 2006, ABC's *World News* ran print ads for its prime time news anchor, Charles Gibson, which said, "Trust Charles Gibson."[6] CNN refers to itself as "the most trusted source in news."

Rockwell Collins, providing electronic communication and aviation solutions, refers to itself as a company that is "building trust every day."[7] This follows a 2004 advertising campaign that stated "Trust Matters."[8]

---

[6] Print advertisement, *US News & World Report*, October 2, 2006.

[7] Print advertisement, *Forbes*, July 4, 2006.

[8] Print advertisement, *BusinessWeek*, September 20, 2004.

Of course trust matters. But it doesn't come so easily that a print ad will create it. Declaring "trust me" does not create trust. It is not what you say; it is what you do that counts.

Provide iconic tangible evidence that what you are claiming can be trusted. Iconic products or services are tangible demonstrations of the truth of your claim. When revitalizing a brand, it is not enough to say, "We are listening to you." "We are changing." Iconic tangible expressions of this claim of change are essential. This is what the launch of a chicken Caesar salad did for McDonald's in April 2003. This is what the relaunch of the Nissan Z did for the Nissan brand in January 2002.

Trust is the conviction that brand will live up to expectations. This means that the promised expectation of the brand can be relied on.

Starbucks promised a special third place—a place away from home or office—a convenient café experience where you could relax alone or sit with friends, savoring a variety of great tasting, personalized, freshly prepared coffees while drinking in great coffee aromas. When that promise became muddled and Starbucks lost touch with its very essence, customers became disappointed. Starbucks lost brand trust. It is taking the return of Howard Schultz to remind the company what the brand is all about.

Remember when United Airlines promised that its skies were friendly? Many customers today probably do not find the trip from Chicago's O'Hare Airport to New York's LaGuardia Airport a friendly experience. Do not overpromise. Promise what you can deliver and deliver what you promise.

Be Predictable

Creating a predictable pattern of behavior is a critical component of trust building. Extraordinary guarantees are a way to foster predictability. Nordstrom built its reputation as a trusted brand by providing unconditional guarantees without question. Lands' End was launched with the simple promise of "Guaranteed. Period."

FedEx built a business on guaranteeing that your letter would be at its destination overnight. To compete, the US Postal Service established an overnight service as well. But over the years, the Postal Service has not lived up to its promised behavior while FedEx has consistently continued to provide overnight, next-morning delivery. Which one do you trust?

Making McDonald's Trustworthy Again

Customers had lost trust in McDonald's. We needed to demonstrate that we were worthy of their trust again. So, we embarked on a series of trust-building activities. Again, it is not what you claim. It is what you do that matters.

Customers wanted new choices to satisfy their evolving dietary desires. In 2003, Jim Cantalupo announced expanded choices for Happy Meals with such items as fruit slices, carrot sticks, fruit juice, water, milk, yogurt beverages, grilled cheese sandwiches, and other items depending on the country.

Reflecting the views of the health community regarding "energy balance" as a critical health factor, McDonald's promoted Bob Greene's walk across America. As Oprah Winfrey's trainer, Bob Greene had become a recognized fitness expert. Canada developed a school program encouraging physical fitness. While encouraging physical fitness among children is an important message, for McDonald's the critical issue is the food. Overemphasis on physical activity over the food as the key message will be viewed as an attempt to excuse McDonald's from being responsible.

In 2003, McDonald's introduced an adult Happy Meal with a new salad, bottled water, and a pedometer. Over time, new menu items such as yogurt parfaits, a grilled chicken salad in China, tuna in the Caribbean, protein platters in Canada, a Japanese vegetarian bagel sandwich, and the Fruit & Walnut Salad in the United States were introduced. McDonald's disbanded "super sizes."

In Australia, by partnering with the highly respected Food Group, McDonald's was soon perceived to be a leader in the important social issue of our food and its effect on health and well-being.

In the UK, with the participation of the BBC, a series of two-minute animated messages were created to entertain and educate children to eat more vegetables.

Happy Meal toys are an important contributor to McDonald's sales. Children love the Happy Meal toys. Parents trust that these toys will be safe. Under the leadership of Peter Schaefer and Rhonda Urbik, in 2004 McDonald's raised its already high specifications for toy safety. Working with Bureau Veritas and Intertek Labs, McDonald's innovated in developing new, higher standards for safety assurance. The McDonald's standards exceed accepted government standards. Safety testing is conducted every step along the way beginning with toy design evaluation through finished product. Even in the 2007-2008 environment of a variety of toy recalls, McDonald's Happy Meal toys can be trusted.

Here's why McDonald's Happy Meal toys are safe. It begins with Rhonda Urbik, McDonald's Director of Safety and Security, who is passionate about the safety of Happy Meal toys. Under her leadership:

- All Happy Meal toys are made exclusively for McDonald's by McDonald's own safety-approved suppliers. They're not "off-the-shelf" toys or made by anyone else.
- When it comes to toy safety, we take nothing for granted. We watch every step of the process. McDonald's toy safety record far exceeds the record for the toy industry overall.
- McDonald's suppliers do not use lead-based paint on Happy Meal toys. This safety step has been a McDonald's mandate for more than 20 years.
- Happy Meal toys are tested time and time again. They're backed by a proactive safety program that starts with the design of the toy and continues throughout the entire process, long before a Happy Meal toy makes it to the production line.

- Testing toys is nothing new at McDonald's. We have been testing and retesting our Happy Meal toys for decades. Testing is performed hourly, daily, or weekly depending on the toy's production cycle. Typically, each year more than 1,000,000 safety tests are conducted on McDonald's toys.

- McDonald's safety process is backed by a team of more than 300 professional injury data analysts, human factor scientists, safety engineers, design engineers, quality engineers, and test engineers around the world.[9]

Actions speak louder than words. When it comes to building trust, customers want to see that you are trustworthy so they can believe that you are trustworthy.

Lead the Debate; Don't Hide from It

Ray Kroc once said: "The leader has got to be willing to take risk, stick his neck out, be optimistic, be progressive."[10]

Staying silent when big issues are at stake is not a signal of leadership. Silence means agreement. Trust is too important for silence. Leaders stand up for what they stand for.

Chipotle is not as big as McDonald's, Wendy's, Burger King, Taco Bell, or KFC. But trust leadership is not about how big you are, but about how big you act. Steve Ells, the founder and CEO of Chipotle, stands up for what he stands for. His personal passion and brand mission is to "change the way people think about and eat fast food."[11]

Steve Ells recognizes the negative connotations of fast food. But, he also knows that the problem with fast food is not that it is fast. He

---

[9] WDTV.com, Breanna Burmeister, May 22, 2007.

[10] Kroc, Ray, 1968 Toronto Leadership Video.

[11] "Chipotle Commits to Serving More Than 50 Million Pounds of Naturally Raised Meat in 2008," *The Wall Street Journal Online*, January 7, 2008; Chipotle Press Release, Chipotle Mexican Grill.

sees the problem with fast food as the food. Steve is proud to serve great food fast. Chipotle is not just creating a better-tasting burrito. Chipotle serves Niman Ranch pork and free-range chicken and uses organic beans and sour cream with no BGH. Chipotle is the largest restaurant buyer of humanely raised meat. Chipotle has committed to suppliers to serve 52 million pounds of naturally raised meat in 2008, a 40% increase over 2007. As Steve Ells stated, "We want to influence the supply chain in the United States."[12]

Steve's personal motto, "food with integrity," is reflected in the entire Chipotle experience. He knows that without genuine integrity, there is no brand credibility. To Steve, brand integrity crosses all aspects of the brand, from how you treat your suppliers to how you treat the environment to how you prepare your food and to how you treat your employees and customers.

Instead of being defensive about serving great food fast, Steve Ells believes that standing up for your principles is serious business and good for business.

Going on the defensive is also a wrong approach. For a brand to be taken seriously, a defensive posture implies that you have something to hide. When you are silent or when you hide, others can create the truths about you. Others will recast your profile. A brand will have a reputation. The only question is who will have the strongest voice in managing that reputation. It is not in a brand's interests to let outsiders trample on a brand's truths.

You must also make sure that all employees understand the key messages. Managers should go through message training, as they did at McDonald's, so if asked by a supplier or if interviewed by the trade press, they each know exactly what to say.

Nike handled the issue of poor factory conditions in Asia not by being silent but by instituting new rules and making visible, vocal

---

[12] Cohen, Arianne, "Ode to a Burrito," *Fast Company*, April 2008.

strides toward changing their overseas manufacturing commitments. Nike did not hide from the problem. It took a visible approach to eliminating the problem. CNBC has a one-hour special on rotation focusing on the Nike brand, the Nike culture, its innovative core, and its remarkable and forthright approach to visibly handling, not hiding, its overseas labor practices.[13]

After 2007's disastrous holiday toy season, a season riddled with recalls, the major toy companies increased their inspections in China. The major toy retailers imposed stricter regulations as well. MEGA Brands, a Canadian toy company that experienced toy-safety issues, working with Intertek Labs has instituted a new safety testing standard that is the highest in the toy industry, exceeding government standards.[14]

The Arrow Is Aimed at Fast Food

The fast food industry, in particular, is a major target in the ongoing global health debates. As the market leader, McDonald's is the poster child for these attacks. McDonald's was criticized and ostracized by commentators, consumer advocate groups, dietary experts, legislators, regulators, lawyers, authors, filmmakers, nongovernmental organizations (NGOs), and others.

As the biggest and most visible fast food company, McDonald's was continually singled out as a major contributor to the global health

---

[13] "SWOOSH! Inside Nike: CNBC presents an unprecedented look inside Nike's $16 Billion Empire," reported and anchored by Darren Rovell, CNBC Sports Reported, CNBC, 2007.

[14] The problems in the toy industry were captured in numerous articles, a sampling of such are: Story, Louise, "Putting Playthings to the Test," *The New York Times*, August, 29, 2007; Morgenstern, Gretchen, "Toy Magnets Attract Sales, And Suits," *The New York Times*, July 15, 2007; Simon, Bernard, "Toy Story with a Tough Moral for Managers," *The Financial Times*, August 9, 2007; Casey, Nicholas, "Toy-Safety Measures Expand," *The Wall Street Journal*, September 11, 2007; Tschang, Chi-Chi, "Bottlenecks in Toyland," *BusinessWeek*, October 15, 2007; McIlroy, Megan, "How Mattel Can Win Back Parents," *Advertising Age*, August 6, 2007.

problem. This is both a penalty of leadership and a benefit of leadership. When a leader speaks, the world listens.

Rather than hide from an issue, lead the debate. Take positive action. Tell your story.

Tell Your Story

When it comes to the debate on important social issues, be an active participator, not a defensive spectator. As some of the negative perceptions of eating fast food took hold, the perception of the food quality became more and more negative. Silence on the issue of McDonald's food was detrimental to the brand. Through a range of initiatives, McDonald's spoke out publicly about the high-quality food it provides its customers.

In Australia, McDonald's engaged in a fully integrated marketing and product development program emphasizing quality and trust. McDonald's Australia was assertive in its public participation as a leader in the important social issue of food and its effect on health and well-being. Guy Russo, managing director, became a respected leader in that country, positioning McDonald's as part of the solution.

In the UK, among other communications, a program using the distribution of 17,000,000 brochures described how McDonald's was changing.

In France, a country where McDonald's kind of food was considered to be contrary to the entire concept of French cuisine, under the leadership of Denis Hennequin, as we said before, McDonald's became a respected business. Like the experience in Australia, Denis did not hide from the debate.

Through an extensive communications program combined with local adaptations to the menu using French foods, McDonald's became a trusted venue. The brand image in France was that McDonald's was a restaurant brand born in America but nurtured in France by the French. Denis's leadership in France was recognized and rewarded with the leadership of Europe. By 2008, Europe was outperforming the United States in sales and earnings growth.[15]

"What I Eat and What I Do"

McDonald's developed and aired an "eat right and stay active" message in a youthful, spirited, contemporary manner. This message headline was "It's what I eat and what I do." This theme tied together various messages in various media including the Internet, local events, and so on. The short phrase instantly communicated in easy to understand language the rather complex concept of energy balance. It is important to both eat right and be active. The entire organization was introduced to the program via a satellite meeting.

"What I eat" comes first because this is the first responsibility of a food company. Focusing only on communicating the need to be more active shifts the whole responsibility to the consumer. Food companies also have a responsibility to help consumers make informed, smarter choices.

PepsiCo demonstrated leadership with its "Smart Spot" program. It is a symbol on more than 250 PepsiCo food and beverages indicating that these products meet the nutrition criteria of the US Food and Drug Administration and the National Academy of Sciences.

Trust leadership is more than just standing out. It requires speaking out. In revitalizing a brand, it is necessary to speak up for your brand if you want your brand to stand out.

---

[15] Gibson, Richard, "McDonald's Profit Rebounds on Strong Overseas Results," *The Wall Street Journal*, April 22, 2008. See also, Kardos, Donna, "McDonald's US Sales Rebound," *The Wall Street Journal*, May 8, 2008, for additional US versus Europe comparisons in results.

Openness Is an Opportunity

Truth is not the same as trust. Truth is a fact. Trust is a feeling. To build your brand into a trustmark, you need both truth and trust. To be worthy of a customer's trust, people need to see the truth not just read about it.

"Without openness, trust is blind." This was a conclusion from the 2003 Brand Council's Business Superbrands survey reported in the February 2004 issue of *Brand Strategy*. The study reported that in the UK managers see openness as a key driver of excellence in brand performance. These managers' responses were interpreted as saying that openness "lifts the veil of secrecy and ambiguity" allowing the customer to see what is going on, and be a part of it if they so choose.[16]

There is a lot of talk about openness today. The April 2007 issue of *Wired* magazine was devoted to this idea. The cover "Get Naked and Rule the World" proclaimed that "Smart companies are sharing secrets with rivals, blogging about products in their pipeline, even admitting to their failures. The name of this new game is 'radical transparency,' and it's sweeping boardrooms across the nation. So strip down and learn how to have it all by baring it all."[17]

Openness is an important aspect of trust-building in a brand revitalization program. Take the McDonald's Open Doors program. This was an idea first developed by Denis Hennequin in France. Teachers, parents, and children became visitors to McDonald's restaurants, viewing the kitchen, seeing how the food is assembled, watching the grills being cleaned and the floors being mopped, having crew members and managers talk about the way the operation is run on a daily basis.

---

[16] Business Superbrands survey, *Brand Strategy*, February 2004; www.superbrands. uk.com; brandstrategy.co.uk; www.accountancyage.com/accountancyage/features/ 2139749/branding-mark.

[17] *Wired*, cover copy, April 2007.

The concept was to literally open the doors of the restaurant for a "behind the scenes" view. The media were invited too. Everyone learned about the food—how it is delivered, prepared, and served. When the program began in France, it raised their corporate earnings.

Openness has its risks. Once you get naked, you had better be in good shape. And, the way things are going now, with Google you are already naked on the Web. Very little secrecy is left.[18] *Advertising Age* followed this story and wrote their own article indicating that mistakes will happen, and transparency means no doctored view.[19]

A recent study by Michael Pirson and Deepak Malhotra also addresses the risks associated with transparency. The authors point out that building trust with one group of constituents may erode trust with another.[20]

Trusted Messages Must Come from a Trustworthy Source

The author Joseph Conrad said the power of sound has always been greater than the power of sense.[21] In reviewing McDonald's communications, we realized that we were making sense, we just sounded wrong. Our voice was wrong for our priority segments.

Trust relies on a relationship of shared values. It relies on a sense of conversation and interaction. Trust is more than having the right argument; it means using the right voice. So, as we discussed previously, we changed the voice of the brand. Customers did not like being talked down to. They did not like being told what to do by a corporate behemoth. Our McDonald's tone of voice was just all wrong for the modern consumer.

---

[18] Ibid.

[19] Creamer, Matthew, "You Call This Transparency?" *Advertising Age*, April 30, 2007.

[20] Pirson, Michael, and Deepak Malhotra, "Unconventional insights for managing stakeholder trust," *MITSloan Management Review* (2008), 49(4): 43-50.

[21] Conrad, Joseph, "A Familiar Preface," *A Personal Record*, Britain, 1912.

Numerous brands today are soliciting customer input as to product innovations and marketing. But it will all be for nothing if the way the customers' ideas are played back to them is in a demeaning or disrespectful tone of voice.

Just as peer testimony is more trustworthy than corporate testimony, the voice of the customer is more trusted than a corporate voice. The decision was to have communications that reflected the most trusted voice: The choice of customers expressing what they love about life and how McDonald's fits into that life.

As mentioned in Chapter 5, "Rule #3: Reinvent the Brand Experience," the concept behind "i'm lovin' it" was that our customers had a forever young attitude, loved life, and loved that McDonald's fit into their life. The "i" reflected the voice of the customer rather than the voice of the corporation. "it" was the distinctive pleasure of the McDonald's experience in their lives.

While peer testimony is the most trusted testimony, expert testimony is also trusted. Customers trust messages that come from trusted outside sources. Crest garnered immediate trust in the 1950s when it received the seal of the American Dental Association (ADA). In Spain, McDonald's received the endorsement of pediatricians.

In Australia, a credible outside consultant was engaged, the Food Group. This is one of Australia's most respected accredited groups of practicing dieticians. They endorsed the new menu items they helped to create.

McDonald's created a Global Advisory Council of experts—doctors, nutritionists, and so forth, all well-respected in their fields—helping McDonald's to address the important issue of obesity, particularly obesity in children.

Providing trustworthy information is critical. The challenge is to become a trustworthy source of information that is helpful, convenient, understandable, and valuable to your customers. Become an open source of information that is understandable, accessible, timely, and trustworthy.

Whole Foods provides information on its philosophy of food and connects consumers to other helpful sites. IKEA has an online responsive helper named Anna. Go online at www.ikea.com and "Ask Anna" for help if you need a new kitchen item or if you need a new kitchen. Petside.com is a wonderful online information resource for pet care. The site answers your questions and provides helpful hints on owning and raising pets.

Good Citizenship Pays

Being a good citizen has many different facets, but at its most basic it is about doing good deeds. There is a huge effort and allocation of resources at the corporate level in the area of doing well (businesswise) by doing good works. And being a good corporate citizen—once a company gets it right—helps the organization deliver enduring profitable growth in a complicated and uncertain world.

The January 19, 2008, issue of *The Economist* ran a special report on corporate social responsibility. The report began by saying that in a world rocked by corporate scandals, trust has eroded.

Because of this, companies work hard today to keep their reputations intact and free from blame. In addition, the article points out that doing good deeds plays a critical part in the hiring of employees and in employee morale: People want to work at a company where their values, ethics, and moralities are in sync with those of the company.[22]

Trust does not come from how big you are. It is a result of how big you act. For example, Starbucks has been visible in its support of programs for Earth Day, Clean Water, and Fair Trade coffee. Procter &

---

[22] Franklin, Daniel, et al., "Just good business: a special report on corporate social responsibility," *The Economist*, January 19, 2008. For full list of acknowledgements, see www.economist.com/specialreports.

Gamble announced in May 2007 that it would reduce packaging for its detergents by selling highly concentrated liquids in smaller containers. All these efforts and the social responsibility efforts of many companies speak to the practicality of building trust through good works.

Building trust through good works means more than mere sponsorship. It is more than a once-a-year promotion supporting a run for breast cancer awareness, an Earth Day event, or an annual Christmas donation. Building trust means integrating commitment to the cause on a sustainable, ongoing basis as a relevant reinforcement of the brand promise.

Consumers want assurances that your motivation is authentic. This means that the cause to which you commit your brand should be tied closely with your brand. Consumers can tell whether your attachment to a cause is opportunistic.

Pedigree Dog Food's support of The Pedigree Adoption Drive is a terrific example of building trust through good works. PepsiCo, with the help of actor Matt Damon, through the Ethos water brand, donates a nickel for every bottle of Ethos water sold, to help children around the world have clean drinking water.

Rebuilding trust is a commitment a brand makes to its customers—and to its employees—on both local and global grounds. Market leaders have a special responsibility and a special opportunity. Market leaders like McDonald's cannot solve a social problem alone. But as market leaders, their market influence is greater than their market share. Market leaders should commit to using their size and strength to set powerful examples for others to follow. If leaders do not lead, then others will attack the leaders for failing in their responsibilities.

Ray Kroc believed that doing the right thing is the right thing to do. He taught that good citizens give back to the community. He had passion about being a responsible citizen, a good neighbor, and a responsible leader.

McDonald's partnered with Conservation International and several suppliers to develop guidelines for prioritizing responsibility in agriculture and food systems covering social, environmental, and animal welfare issues. McDonald's has been a vocal advocate of beef safety through certification from farm to your plate. The decision was made to not purchase beef from the rain forests or recently deforested rain areas. McDonald's has supported elimination of several torturous practices in the chicken and pork industries. The company pursues an environmentally sound fish sourcing strategy.[23]

For decades, McDonald's has supported children in need through the Ronald McDonald House where the families of seriously ill children can live during the course of pediatric hospital stays. World Children's Day was created as an annual day dedicated to the well-being of children and has raised millions of dollars for children's charities. In addition to World Children's Day other programs, such as the Ronald McDonald Care Mobile program and the broader Ronald McDonald House Charities, offer helping hands to children in need.

McDonald's also has a heritage of local community involvement. Ray Kroc insisted that giving back to and becoming a part of the local neighborhood surrounding the restaurant was essential. "We should cooperate with the civic group and the community group in whatever is going on. If they need a new playground, if they need new playground equipment, we should do what we can to cooperate with them. We want their business. And, it's not enough to just want their business to have them come over to our place and leave the money there. We've got to do something about making them feel friendlier towards us. And...wanting to come to our place because we are cognizant of the community and we show a spirit of cooperation. We have an obligation to give back to the community that gives so much to us."[24]

---

[23] McDonald's Worldwide Corporate Responsibility Report, 2004 and 2006.
[24] Kroc, Ray, *Phil Donahue Show*, 1977.

Trust building is a major challenge for business, but the rewards are well worth it. At McDonald's, we learned that trust could be rebuilt. It takes time and effort; it takes commitment, but it pays.[25]

The Do's and Don'ts of Rebuilding Trust

Do

- **Build trust measures into your Scorecard**—Trust can be measured. If you do not know the degree to which your customers trust your brand, you are headed into brand triage.

- **Become part of the solution for your customers' important issues**—Customers prefer brands reflecting values that match their own. You do not want customers who say, "Great brand, but it just isn't me."

- **Behave predictably**—Erratic behavior and changing beliefs and values confuse customers and dilute trust. Allow your customers to become familiar with you, your values, and behaviors. Familiarity breeds comfort.

- **Provide information**—If you do not, the customers will find it anyway. The Internet is an image-maker or an image-breaker.

- **Reevaluate the tonality and voice of your communications**—Communications that talk down to or demean customers may be funny and witty, but you may be insulting someone.

- **Seek out credible third-party testimony**—Borrowing credibility is acceptable. The halo effect may be just the thing your brand needs to rebuild trust. If your trust has run off, let someone else's trust rub off on you.

---

[25] People are loyal to trustworthy brands, and building brand loyalty pays off. Fredrick Reichheld reported that a bank found that a 5% increase in customer retention grew that company's profits by 60%. In the life of an insurance company, a 5% increase in customer retention lowered costs per policy by 18%. Reichheld, Frederick F., "Loyalty-Based Management," *Harvard Business Review*, March/April 1993.

- **Become involved**—Whether locally, globally, or both, find issues that show you care and then participate. In your customers' eyes, you are what you do.

Don't

- **Don't just talk, DO**—Actions speak louder than words. Demonstrate; don't just discuss.
- **Don't overpromise**—Promise what you can deliver and deliver what you promise. Setting up expectations that you cannot meet will help disintegrate trust.
- **Don't be silent**—Silence may be golden but only if you are in the library reading room. Speak up for your brand. State your goals. People need to hear what you have to say.
- **Don't hide**—Smoke screens do not provide comfort, they create cover-ups. Customers want to know the truth. As Loren Baritz writes in his book, *Backfire*, "A secret is a private truth and that is an acceptable definition of madness."[26]

---

[26] Baritz, Loren, *Backfire: A History of How American Culture Led Us into Vietnam and Made Us Fight the Way We Did*, Baltimore: Johns Hopkins University Press, 1998.

8

Rule #6: Realize Global Alignment

"None of us are as good as all of us."[1] Working together works best was always a principle driving Ray Kroc. He believed that everyone worked first and foremost for the system and in so doing would be working for individual success. He believed that you are in business for yourself, as an entrepreneur, but that you were not working by yourself.

For Ray Kroc, for McDonald's, and for any organization working for the greatness of their brand(s), alignment is everything.

The rules-based practices for realizing global alignment are as follows:

- Execute the Plan to Win
- Establish Freedom Within a Framework

Alignment

Alignment means we are working together toward the same destination. We all have the same brand purpose and brand promise as our goals. We have the same view as to where the brand is headed. We have the same common definition of brand priorities. We have the same common metrics.

---

[1] Kroc, Ray, Corporate Motto, 1979.

Freedom Within a Framework facilitates global consistency while maintaining local relevance. The Plan to Win is an important tool in helping to ensure global alignment.

Freedom Within a Framework

Being aligned does not mean being an automaton. Brand alignment does not limit creativity. It focuses the creative process.

The great legal expert Charles Louis Montesquieu said, "Liberty is the right of doing whatever the laws permit." He added that, "Liberty has rules; otherwise it would be anarchy."[2]

A global brand revitalization initiative needs to assure everyone that just because we were committing to common focus and organizational alignment sharing a common Plan to Win, this did not mean an end to creative thinking. In fact, it was the opposite. We were encouraging creative liberty. But, we created some laws to guide our creativity.

Our view is that global alignment is not about global marketing standardization. It is about global marketing harmonization. Our policy of Freedom Within a Framework liberates us to be relevant to local market conditions while ensuring that we communicate with local brand voices that communicate and resonate in powerful brand harmony worldwide.

But Freedom Within a Framework goes beyond just marketing communications, like the Plan to Win went beyond marketing. It affects everything. Freedom Within a Framework means that you create some boundaries. People are encouraged to have freedom to be creative within the defined boundaries. You are not allowed to go out and shift the boundaries anymore than you are allowed to go out and shift the border between New York and Pennsylvania, or

---

[2] Montesquieu, Charles Louis de Secondat, *The Spirit of Laws*, France, 1748.

between Germany and France. But within the defined brand boundaries, you have a lot of leeway.

Focus

Global alignment requires focus. As you can imagine, for a huge brand marketed in more than 100 countries with 47 million customers per day, focus is not easy to achieve. A lot of people think that focus is limiting. Freedom Within a Framework was criticized for providing boundaries that were described as limiting. But focus is not limiting; focus is strengthening. Organizational focus and alignment are fundamental to marketing a powerful brand.

McDonald's achieved clear brand and business focus. As indicated earlier, the new business-building focus changed from growing by putting more stores in front of customers to growing by attracting more customers to its stores.

It sounds so simple, yet it was an enormous change and presented a challenge internally and to Wall Street. Growth through growing the number of restaurants is easier to see; it is more visible: new location, new geography, new restaurant, and new numbers. Focus on organic growth is easy to say, but not easy to do.

This is why the Plan to Win is so important. The new brand purpose provided focus. Instead of focusing on sales at any cost, McDonald's focused on increasing sales by becoming the customer's favorite place and way to eat.

The new brand promise articulated as Forever Young provided a coherent new brand direction that guided all the marketing worldwide. Everything implemented on behalf of the brand was focused using the lens of Forever Young and its defined dimensions.

How do you achieve organizational commitment? Internal marketing must precede external marketing. An effective internal marketing effort requires that we address four internal question areas:

- **Education**—What are the new brand purpose and brand promise all about? Why are we doing it? Why now?
- **Inspiration**—What kind of future will we create? Why should I believe? Is the leadership truly committed? Are management behaviors consistent with the Plan to Win?
- **Implementation**—What does this all mean to me? What are we going to do differently? What am I expected to do differently? Will support be provided?
- **Evaluation**—How will we measure and manage progress? Will we recognize and reward those who produce the right results the right way?

> **Four Elements of Internal Marketing**
>
> - Education
> - Inspiration
> - Implementation
> - Evaluation

Internal Marketing Is a Must

Internal marketing is not just a way to ensure that the concepts of Freedom Within a Framework and the Plan to Win are inculcated into behaviors and attitudes.

Internal marketing is more than mere internal communication. It is not enough to just communicate the management message. We must apply the same external marketing skills to our internal audiences.

Internal marketing defines business and personal success for the brand revitalization. This is critical. People need to know what is expected and on what basis they will be evaluated and compensated.

When a brand is under attack, an effective internal marketing program revitalizes the spirit of employees helping them to feel comfortable and proud to work for the brand.

In the 1980s at Mars, associates were finding it difficult to defend the fact that they worked for a "candy" company. Mars spent time, effort, and resources developing and implementing ongoing programs about nutrients, diet, oral hygiene, and the composition of their high-quality anytime foods. They produced booklets and videos. The goal was to assist associates in food knowledge. People who worked at Mars should be informed as to the basics of nutrition and oral hygiene. The result was that associates who were parents could respond to their kids' teachers on why a Milky Way bar might be in a lunch box. The result was that associates could converse at a cocktail party and not feel embarrassed; they had credible responses to give. This type of education builds pride. It made every associate an advocate for the brands.

General Electric has an extraordinary commitment to executive education. I have participated in several of these seminar programs. The GE education not only provides knowledge and best-case internal and external practices, but also creates a common ground for executive discussions and behaviors.

At Nissan, not only were all employees schooled in the new brand promise, but dealers were given a course as well. Dealerships were reimaged. A brand book and a frequently asked questions booklet were created and distributed globally. A video featuring Carlos Ghosn was created, as was a video bringing the target customer to life.

McDonald's needed the support of 1.6 million employees. To revitalize the attitude of employees, an extensive global internal campaign was launched to introduce the new "i'm lovin' it" campaign to employees before it was launched externally. The response was overwhelming.

In China, the team developed an "i'm lovin' it" hand-signal that was used by crew members to welcome customers in our restaurants. They also developed an "i'm lovin' it" dance that was performed in stores.

Jim Cantalupo and Charlie Bell visited Shanghai and experienced this remarkable surge of energy. On their return, they told me that they could not recall the last time they saw such enthusiasm, pride, and motivation in our people. And the people in China tell me they cannot recall a performance like Jim Cantalupo trying to perform the "i'm lovin' it" dance.

There were joyous crew rallies in Latin America that were simply amazing. The underlying concept of the internal marketing was to turn 1.6 million employees into 1.6 million brand ambassadors.

Internal marketing is always challenging, but the rewards are encouraging, sometimes spectacular. People continually ask me how we were able to get all 119 countries in the McDonald's universe to launch the same brand campaign in the same month in the same way. It was not easy. Instead of behaving like a huge slow battleship, the now revitalized, big McDonald's brand turned like a sailboat in an important race to the future.

Internal marketing gave people a business model that focused on growing organically; convinced them that what they did really mattered; provided a framework for behavior and creativity; encouraged seeking creative ideas from around the world.

Internal marketing helped people deal with the changes that were taking place. Most people are uncomfortable with change. It helped people step out of their comfort zone and become active participators in the brand revitalization.

The Do's and Don'ts of Realizing Global Alignment

Do

- **Inform everybody**—If you expect people to behave in a certain way, you need to let them know what is going on. As the

New York Times said in May 1986, "Secrecy is a disease, and Chernobyl is its symptom."[3] Tell people what is expected.

- **Create a sense of urgency**—Most people will wait for that piece of research or the new campaign or the financial savior. There may be miracle workers in business, but getting people to start moving forward fast is a critical first step.

- **Define success**—Let people know what the winning hand will be. Explain and aim for understanding so everyone knows it when they grasp the gold ring.

- **Provide educational opportunities**—Train, coach, and teach people so they can perform and change attitudes.

- **Measure progress**—People manage what they believe management measures. And they need to see progress so as not to feel defeated.

- **Learn from failure**—Continuous improvement is the mantra. It is okay to fail as long as you learn from it and figure out how to improve.

- **Recognize and reward genuine progress**—Always celebrate the small success, provide feedback, and give people incentives to move forward.

Don't

- **Don't say we can't**—Starting off with negatives is not an incentive for anyone. Alignment will be easier if you repeat, "I think I can. I think I can."

- **Don't remain in the comfort zone**—Change makes people uncomfortable. That is to be expected. If you are too comfortable, it probably means that you are doing the same thing or doing nothing.

- **Don't just talk**—Just "talking the talk" will not bring about alignment. You must speak and do at the same time. Actions speak louder than words. Declarations must be backed up with deeds.

---

[3] Editorial page, "Mayday! and May Day," *The New York Times*, May 1, 1986, Section A, p. 26, Column 1.

9

Realizing Global Alignment: Creating a Plan to Win

How many times have you heard management say, "We all need to be on the same page"? That phrase, "on the same page," seems to be the Holy Grail for marketers, managers, and executive teams regardless of the type of business. Yet rarely do organizations create that "one page" of purpose, actions, and metrics to which all can adhere. A Plan to Win (PTW) does just that: It puts the purpose, promise, actions, and performance metrics on a single page so that everyone can be on the same page.

The purpose of the PTW is to achieve organizational alignment. It is so important for brand revitalization that I am devoting this chapter to explaining how to create one.

For brand revitalization, we need to change the brand culture from playing not to lose, to committing to a roadmap that defines how we will win.

The PTW ensures the integration of brand actions across the Eight Ps: Purpose, Promise, People, Product, Place, Price, Promotion, and Performance.

In Chapter 3, "Rule #1: Refocus the Organization," we emphasized that people need a sense of purpose: They want to know that their work makes a difference. What is the shared sense of purpose, the common direction that will align us all? To revitalize a brand, we need to refocus and re-inspire the organization around a common sense of purpose.

The PTW begins with defining the brand purpose and brand promise. This means answering these questions: What are we trying to achieve and what is the promised experience for our customers?

Brand purpose is the first P in our PTW. A brand purpose is a compelling statement of the overarching brand intent or mission. It must define a clear sense of direction, an overarching goal for the organization and the brand.

Brand promise is the second P in our PTW. The brand promise is the contract we make with our customers. It summarizes that special bond between the customer and brand and expresses the promise that if you buy our brand, you will get a distinctive brand experience.

In Chapter 4, "Rule #2: Restore Brand Relevance," we described the necessity of restoring relevance to the McDonald's brand. We redefined the differentiating brand experience we wanted to promise and deliver.

Brand purpose and brand promise provide the focused direction for the PTW. Once the purpose and promise are defined, what are the actions we will take to deliver the brand promise to achieve the brand purpose? Effectiveness of a brand purpose and promise are not determined by good intentions. Effectiveness is achieved by the actions we take.

This brings us to the five action Ps—people, products, place, price, and promotion. The five action Ps define how we will deliver our brand promise to yield more customers, more often, more brand loyalty, and more profit.

These define our action priorities for bringing the brand promise to life. Brand revitalization means reinvention across all the five action Ps. In Chapter 5, "Rule #3: Reinvent the Brand Experience," we described these five action Ps in detail.

Creating a results culture means creating a culture that is evaluated based on producing measurable results. In Chapter 6, "Rule #4: Reinforce a Results Culture," we reviewed the imperative of defining measurable milestones and rewarding people based on business and brand performance.

At McDonald's, we designed and implemented a global systemwide measurement program. Annual milestones spanning three years were created to monitor progress.[1] Charlie Bell was personally committed to measuring progress on a regular basis. Charlie maintained an up-to-date board in his office that displayed the Brand Scorecard results for all to see.

Measures included items relating to the five action Ps, such as changes in employee commitment, product perceptions, and brand strength.

With the PTW as the brand roadmap, all business units would be aligned around the same goals, actions, and measures. This was not by any means a small gesture. Creating a PTW requires top management visible and verbal support. This is essential. Anything that affects how people are evaluated and compensated is a volatile issue. Top management must deliver the clarion call for alignment and be the leaders of the inspiration that will affect behaviors.

To alleviate some of this reluctance to work from a common set of guidelines and standards, it is imperative to set a realistic and workable timetable. When people are asked to "get on board," that means now. This train has a schedule.

Here is a summary of the benefits of galvanizing the organization behind a common PTW:

- A Plan to Win is a common platform for rebuilding brand value. It provides the necessary list of priorities for success. A Plan to Win creates the platform for renewal.
- A Plan to Win outlines the critical brand components from purpose and promise through the five action areas to the measurement of progress. Inconsistent business and brand

---

[1] As noted previously, the Shareholder Brochure from October 2003 included details of the Plan to Win and the measurement goals.

building creates internal global chaos. People should have the freedom to do what is best locally within the global framework.

- A Plan to Win creates a common clarity encouraging everyone to aim in the same direction by having the same brand goals and priorities. You cannot be successful if you are unfocused. Focus is fundamental.

- A Plan to Win helps an organization act as an integrated global team breaking down functional and geographic silos. Isolationism is limiting: It stifles creative thinking by limiting return on global learning.

The Three Sections of the Plan to Win

A Plan to Win has three sections:

- **Section 1: Brand Direction**—This section articulates the brand purpose and brand promise. Brand purpose answers the questions "Why does this brand exist? And what is the overarching goal of the brand?"

- **Section 2: Brand Action**—The PTW defines the priority actions for implementing the brand direction. These activities are called the five action Ps: people, product, place, price, and promotion. The PTW defines the high-priority activities defined for each of the Ps.

- **Section 3: Brand Performance**—The measurable milestones need to be clearly defined. These metrics will be used to evaluate the progress toward the achievement of the brand purpose and brand promise through implementation of the activities of the five action Ps.

The Plan To Win

- **Brand Direction**—Brand purpose and brand promise
- **Brand Action**—People, product, place, price, and promotion
- **Brand Performance**—Measurable milestones

There are two critical components for doing this well. First, you must have a passionate, dedicated group in top management. Jim Cantalupo, Charlie Bell, and Matt Paull provided this leadership commitment.

Second, achieving organizational alignment behind the brand destination is critical to brand success. This means alignment across functions and across geographies.

KIDDO Garden Foods

To illustrate what a Plan to Win might look like, we created an example for a hypothetical fresh food purveyor (see Figure 9.1).

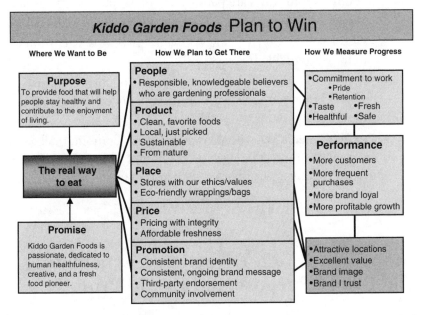

Figure 9.1   Example: Kiddo Garden Foods Plan to Win

The brand's purpose states: "Our dream is that people stay healthy and genuinely enjoy living." This is not a generic statement. It reflects a vision for the future...a vision about people and how they can live their lives.

The brand promises that it is passionate and dedicated to human healthfulness; that it is creative and is a pioneer in the marketplace of fresh food. This is captured in its brand essence: the real way to eat.

To bring this promise to life and make progress toward the vision, the five action Ps create the tasks that must be completed. So, for example:

- **People**—The people at Kiddo Garden Foods are responsible, knowledgeable believers who are gardening professionals.
- **Product**—Our fruits and vegetables are clean, favorite foods that are local, just picked, grown and handled sustainably, and from nature (meaning non-genetically modified organism [GMO], organically grown, and so on).
- **Place**—Our fruits and vegetables are sold in stores that share our ethical values and are packaged with wrappings or bags that are eco-friendly.
- **Price**—We support pricing with integrity so that customers can have affordable freshness.
- **Promotion**—We will have a consistent identity, a consistent ongoing brand message, with third-party endorsement and the support of community involvement.
- **Performance**—We will measure progress both internally and externally so there are measures for both. Kiddo Garden Foods will also conduct third-party safety testing on its products.

How do we put all of this together? What are the specific steps?

Step One: Brand Direction—Articulating the Brand Purpose and Brand Promise

Begin with a desktop review of pertinent information. This will start the process of answering the question: What do we know? The recommended desktop review helps evaluate the current situation. Examine, analyze, and synthesize the following kinds of information:

- Who are the customers in terms of their values, attitudes, beliefs, and so on? How do they feel about the category and the brands in the competitive set and our brand(s)?

- Data on customer perceptions of the brand. Problems? Drivers of choice.

- Is there a segmentation of any sort? What are the customer needs?

- Market dynamics information. Strengths. Weaknesses. Trends.

- Loyalty dynamics.

- Purchase/contractual behavior.

- As much as possible on competition including annual reports, tracking data, and so on.

- Briefs issued at critical periods of time by founder, succeeding chairperson, and management.

- Any brand guidelines that exist. Anything from HQ to local operation regarding brand. Any local brand briefs.

- Any books written about the brand or the company's history.

- Corporate vision/mission? A report of the work that led to this vision.

- Large macro environmental information such as broad social, economic, political, or cultural issues/trends that may have impact on brands.

- Any/all brand positioning statements and creative briefs. Reports, presentations, research, and other information that led to this direction.

- Catalogues; point of sales materials; advertising, promotional, logos, and public relations materials on corporation and individual products.

- What were the most effective campaigns/advertising/PR/other in the brand's history? How did these depict the brand's essence?

- Speeches by key, senior management and all media for last several years that reflect vision, values, and mission for the company.

As mentioned earlier, synthesizing information requires a different sort of person than just any research analyst. You will need a person who can see patterns and commonalities and be able to draw conclusions from whatever evidence is available no matter how fragmentary or intangible.

Follow the desktop review with executive interviews. These can be conducted in person or over the phone depending on geography, time, and money. The interview must be designed to capture the executive's strategic intent for the brand and to fully understand the brand in the context of the specific project. Our aim is to develop a brand vision that will lead to brand revitalization.

The information from the review and the output of the interviews are combined. The synthesis of these interviews along with the information of the review will be the basis for the creation of the new brand purpose.

This brand purpose defines the future we want to create in which our brand will win. So, it is crucial not only to know where we are but also to clearly articulate what we see as the brand destination we will create.

This process defines the brand purpose and the definition of the brand promise.

Step Two: Creating the Five Action Ps

The five action Ps are the actions we must take to accomplish the mission articulated in our brand purpose and to bring our brand to life as defined in the brand promise.

In other words, the brand actions define the boundaries within which local markets are encouraged to be creative. Within the defined boundary lines we encourage creative, free-thinking thought and expression. We call this Freedom Within a Framework. We discussed freedom with in a framework and how this relates specifically to creativity of communications and marketing in Chapter 8, "Rule #6: Realize Global Alignment."

By knowing the organization and the stretch limits and by knowing the product capabilities whether it be manufacturing or gardening or distribution, you will be able to define those specific priority actions necessary for delivering the promise and achieving the mission.

Step Three: Performance Measures

Performance measures can be a challenge, especially if measures are already established for calibrating such things as satisfaction, purchase intent, delivery of quality, or trust. In a global company, each country will support its own measures and phraseology. Each country will tell you that it has normative data. At McDonald's, each country agreed that just as McDonald's had common measures for financial performance, McDonald's should also have common measures for brand performance. However, these same countries each advocated that everyone else should adopt how they do it in their country.

A cross-geography team of researchers will have to review the agreed mission, agreed promise, and the deliverables of the five action Ps and generate the best common internal and external measures that will represent the brand part of the Balanced Scorecard as discussed in Chapter 6.

Implications of a Plan to Win

Enduring profitable growth is the fundamental goal of business. Becoming profitable by reducing costs, eliminating waste, and increasing productivity is important, but it is not a sustainable business growth strategy. It is a cliché, but it is true: You cannot cost-manage your way to the future.

Cost cutting is not really a strategy for enduring prosperity. It is a strategy for profitable management of inevitable decline. We cannot have sustainable growth of the bottom line unless we create quality growth of the top line. To have quality revenue growth, we must profitably create more customers, convince them to come more often, and persuade them to be more brand loyal. The only way to enduring profitable growth is by achieving a sustainable brand advantage that profitably increases customer-perceived value.

Returning Brand Value

At the foundation of the McDonald's Plan to Win was the imperative to rebuild the brand value of McDonald's.

Rebuilding brand value:

- Increases purchase consideration (attractiveness and retention)
- Increases willingness to try more products
- Reduces the cost of marketing innovations
- Decreases price sensitivity
- Increases margins

The Do's and Don'ts of Creating a Plan to Win

Do

- **Create a workable timetable**—Calendar management is tricky, but it is a component of making this work. Create a time frame and do your utmost to stick to it. Don't relax the schedule unless there is a real emergency.

- **Find a creative person, a synthesizing mind**—There is more than just straight reporting going on during this project. You will need the perceptions and intuitions of a synthesizer, creative-type.

- **Find as much pertinent information as possible**—This may require finding those internal people who know where everything is buried. Remember not everything is electronic. In some cases, you will need the vocal support of a top manager to ensure that less interested people send you their materials.

Don't

- **Don't dumb down your brand purpose and brand promise**—These are meant to inspire, creating believers. Simple and clear phrasing does not mean that you write as if your audience cannot read.
- **Don't allow regional or geographic leaders to opt out**—Of course, every country has differences. But we are all part of the same brand mission and are driven to have our brand succeed. We have commonalities; we have things that we must do in common to generate and sustain brand health.
- **Don't overlook potential interviewees just because they are far away or retired**—Some of the most compelling information we collected at McDonald's came from those who had worked with Ray Kroc and were now retired.
- **Don't allow regional or geographic leaders to hide behind "we have norms" and "my country is different"**—Of course, everyone has been collecting data over the years, but there are some commonalities, and we should search for these when dealing with the concepts of quality, trust, satisfaction, and so on.

10

Do the Six Rules of Revitalization Work?

The Six Rules are more than just a set of principles and a set of practices. These Six Rules and the associated practices help to create a proven mindset. Brands can be turned around and brought to life again through adherence to these rules:

- **Rule #1**—Refocus the Organization
- **Rule #2**—Restore Brand Relevance
- **Rule #3**—Reinvent the Brand Experience
- **Rule #4**—Reinforce a Results Culture
- **Rule #5**—Rebuild Brand Trust
- **Rule #6**—Realize Global Alignment

When people work together and move in the same direction toward the same destination with passion and pride, things fall into place. In January 2005, *The New York Times* reported that McDonald's worldwide growth at restaurants open at least 13 months, or same-store sales, was at its highest level in 17 years. Same-store sales grew 5.1 percent in the quarter.[1]

McDonald's won the prestigious *Advertising Age* award as Marketer of the Year in 2004 and was named a top marketer of the year by *BrandWeek* in 2004. In 2005, McDonald's won the Promotion Marketing Association of America (PMAA) Gold Medal and a Gold

---

[1] Warner, Melanie, "Sales Growth at McDonald's Is the Highest in 17 Years," *The New York Times*, January 29, 2005.

Reggie for the best global promotion for the Big Mac promotion with Sony Connect. Many local and regional awards also were won around the world. All these accolades combined with the increased sales and profits that are still growing today point to a reenergized McDonald's brand.

In 2006, McDonald's was awarded the prestigious Effie for effective global advertising for 2005. Here is what the Effie award said about McDonald's:

> Going into 2003, McDonald's business was slumping around the world. Brand relevance was fading. A key factor in turning the business around was the development and implementation of a global advertising campaign, born out of McDonald's brand essence of enduring youthfulness, fun, and vitality. The campaign revitalized customers' emotional connection, creating more positive feelings about the brand.[2]

The consumer responded to McDonald's new brand direction. Marketing experts judged McDonald's brand plans and actions as a laudable marketing success. And the financial community appreciated the effect that the revitalization of the McDonald's brand had on the bottom line. The share price changed from a low of around 13 early in 2003 to 32.06 by the end of 2005.[3]

The combination of a powerful, focused Plan to Win produced remarkable results. Aiming to be our customers' favorite, and aiming to be bigger by being better, worked. In 2004, Jim Cantalupo said, "Our performance last year proved one thing...better run restaurants, better tasting food, better value, and better marketing drives comparable sales, profits, and margins."[4]

---

[2] Effie Award, 2006. See description of the Effie Awards and the committees at www.effie.org.

[3] MSN Stock Charting, www.msn.com.

[4] Cantalupo, Jim, remarks at an analyst meeting, New York City, March 8, 2004.

Moving Forward

In the Preface, I describe the untimely deaths of Jim Cantalupo and Charlie Bell. Jim died at the beginning of the McDonald's Convention in Orlando in 2004, right before he was scheduled to stand up before franchisees, suppliers, and employees and show how the Plan to Win was working. Charlie Bell, who became McDonald's CEO at Jim's death, soon succumbed to colon cancer.

After the unfortunate deaths of Jim Cantalupo and Charlie Bell, the board appointed Jim Skinner as the CEO. Jim Skinner recognized that a management change did not necessarily mean a strategy change. He affirmed his commitment to the strategy he inherited from Cantalupo and Bell. Rather than make changes for the sake of making changes, he committed to continuing and living with Jim Cantalupo's view of becoming bigger by being better. To this day, he continues to execute the Plan to Win developed through the leadership of Cantalupo and Bell.

The Plan to Win not only helped to turn around the business, it also created positive momentum that continued to produce positive results. On November 13, 2007, Matthew Paull, CFO, said, "Our 1-year and 3-year returns on incremental invested capital are roughly double our high-teens targets." McDonald's planned to be more aggressive in opening new stores. But the capital investment would be balanced between existing stores and new stores. According to Matt Paull, "Half of our 2008 cap ex will be used to reinvest in our existing restaurants, and the rest will be primarily used to build about 1,000 new restaurants."[5]

---

[5] "McDonald's to Investors: Plan to Win Positions Company for Future Success," *PR Newswire*, November 13, 2007, http://news.moneycentral.msn.com.

It can be accomplished. A brand can be revitalized. It takes time, effort, and money. It takes energy and people. It takes commitment, and as Charlie Bell would often say, it takes pride and passion. It takes belief.

There is no question that brand revitalization is a challenge. You will face the naysayers who will tell you that it is all a wasted effort. But actually it is a waste of effort to merely reproduce what worked in the past. To revitalize a brand, you must create new basics. Winners create the future; they do not just try to survive in the future.

As the Six Rules of Revitalization demonstrate, revitalization focuses on creating the future, where we want to be, and then implementing our way there.

Summary: Brand Revitalization

Brand revitalization drives financial management, service management, personnel management, product development, distribution management, pricing strategy, marketing management, and operations. Brand becomes the business driver. And the business of everyone is to drive enduring profitable growth of the brand to ever-greater heights.

As we regularly read in the press, when companies fall into holes of their own digging they tend to say that either a new advertising agency is needed or new research is necessary. These are often not solutions. Creating new advertisements without addressing the real underlying problems may be fun, but it will not produce great marketplace results.

More consumer research is often an excuse to delay or abdicate responsibility for creating a new brand vision. Brand vision is the responsibility of the leadership. Consumer research cannot see the future. It can tell you where you are and how you got here. The only future you can predict is the one you create for your brand.

It is not research or advertising: It is brand leadership that revitalizes a brand.

Having a new brand direction is more important than a new slogan. There is no substitute for the power of a clear and consistent definition of a new brand direction and destination. This applies to any brand, whether a troubled brand or a successful brand, new brand or mature brand, big brand or small brand.

The Plan to Win provides clarity of direction. It puts every part of the organization on the same page. Charlie used to call it "aligning for action." He and Jim Cantalupo viewed organizational alignment as an enormous benefit to be harnessed. Their years at McDonald's demonstrated the power that McDonald's, properly aligned, could wield. Organizational alignment:

- Provides clarity of purpose.
- Defines a common brand and business vision.
- Moves the organization toward the same destination.
- Sets priorities.
- Ensures brand consistency across geography and time.
- Defines common goals and measurable objectives.

Following the Six Rules of Revitalization and the rules-based practices, illustrated in Figure 10.1, while creating, implementing, and adhering to a Plan to Win may not be the complete answer for a brand in trouble, but these were implemented at McDonald's as well as other companies. These rules have proven to be a winning combination.

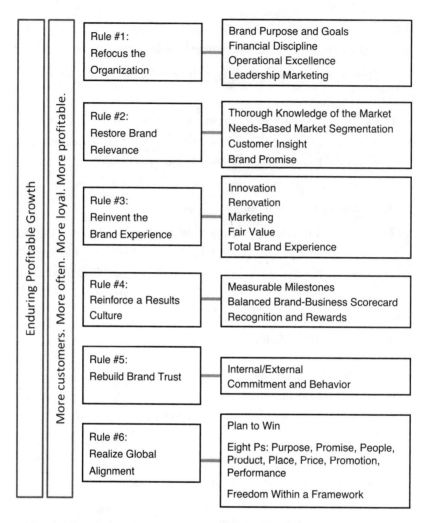

Figure 10.1   Six Rules of Brand Revitalization

INDEX

◖◖ Wharton School Publishing

In the face of accelerating turbulence and change, business leaders and policy makers need new ways of thinking to sustain performance and growth.

Wharton School Publishing offers a trusted source for stimulating ideas from thought leaders who provide new mental models to address changes in strategy, management, and finance. We seek out authors from diverse disciplines with a profound understanding of change and its implications. We offer books and tools that help executives respond to the challenge of change.

Every book and management tool we publish meets quality standards set by The Wharton School of the University of Pennsylvania. Each title is reviewed by the Wharton School Publishing Editorial Board before being given Wharton's seal of approval. This ensures that Wharton publications are timely, relevant, important, conceptually sound or empirically based, and implementable.

To fit our readers' learning preferences, Wharton publications are available in multiple formats, including books, audio, and electronic.

To find out more about our books and management tools, visit us at whartonsp.com and Wharton's executive education site, exceed.wharton.upenn.edu.

Wharton
UNIVERSITY of PENNSYLVANIA

Pearson
Education